D1714638

William Faulkner's

Absalom, Absalom!

Text by
Carol Siri Johnson
(Ph.D. City of New York Graduate Center)
and
Laurie Kalmanson
(M.A. University of Chicago)

Illustrations by
Ann Tango-Schurmann

Research & Education Association

Library of Congress Catalog Card Number 96-67438

International Standard Book Number 0-87891-000-X

What **MAXnotes**® *Will Do for You*

This book is intended to help you absorb the essential contents and features of William Faulkner's *Absalom, Absalom!* and to help you gain a thorough understanding of the work. The book has been designed to do this more quickly and effectively than any other study guide.

For best results, this **MAXnotes** book should be used as a companion to the actual work, not instead of it. The interaction between the two will greatly benefit you.

To help you in your studies, this book presents the most up-to-date interpretations of every section of the actual work, followed by questions and fully explained answers that will enable you to analyze the material critically. The questions also will help you to test your understanding of the work and will prepare you for discussions and exams.

Meaningful illustrations are included to further enhance your understanding and enjoyment of the literary work. The illustrations are designed to place you into the mood and spirit of the work's settings.

The **MAXnotes** also include summaries, character lists, explanations of plot, and section-by-section analyses. A biography of the author and discussion of the work's historical context will help you put this literary piece into the proper perspective of what is taking place.

The use of this study guide will save you the hours of preparation time that would ordinarily be required to arrive at a complete grasp of this work of literature. You will be well prepared for classroom discussions, homework, and exams. The guidelines that are included for writing papers and reports on various topics will prepare you for any added work which may be assigned.

The **MAXnotes** will take your grades "to the max."

Dr. Max Fogiel
Program Director

Contents

Section One: *Introduction* 1

The Life and Work of William Faulkner 1

Historical Background 5

Master List of Characters 6

Chronology 8

Summary of the Novel 10

Estimated Reading Time 13

> **Each Chapter includes List of Characters, Summary, Analysis, Study Questions and Answers, and Suggested Essay Topics.**

Section Two: *Absalom, Absalom!* 15

Chapter 1 15

Chapter 2 23

Chapter 3 30

Chapter 4 37

Chapter 5 46

Chapter 6 52

Chapter 7 60

Chapter 8 68

Chapter 9 74

Section Three: *Sample Analytical Paper Topics* 80

Section Four: *Bibliography* 85

Introduction

The Life and Work of William Faulkner

William Faulkner is arguably one of the greatest American writers from the South. He published 30 books during his lifetime, winning a National Book Award, a Legion of Honor award, the Howells Medal for distinguished fiction, the Gold Medal for Fiction, two Pulitzer Prizes, and, finally, a Nobel prize.

But Faulkner did not lead a completely happy life. As the eldest of four sons, he felt responsible for his entire family. His improvident father drank heavily, as Faulkner did when he became an adult. Moreover, Faulkner's family had owned slaves, and Faulkner felt the weight of guilt of a society whose economic standard was created by the exploitation of others. The burden of the past was heavy upon him; much of Faulkner's writing attempts to come to terms with this past.

William Faulkner's great-grandfather, William Clark Falkner, was a tough frontiersman who ran away from home at a young age, started a plantation in Mississippi, and fought in the Civil War. He lived a violent and active life: he killed two men in feuds, had a large family, ran for public office, and wrote a bestseller, *The White Rose of Memphis* (1880). Eventually, he was killed by a man who bore him a grudge.

Faulkner's grandfather, John Wesley, was more conservative: he made his family fortune in railroads, and he was wounded in a feud. Faulkner's father, Murry, grew up in the shadow of these two strong men: Murry held a secure job on the railroads until his father sold his shares and set his son adrift. After that, Murry didn't know quite what to do, so he drank.

Moreover, all three men, Faulkner's father, grandfather, and great-grandfather, were visited with a legacy of violence: William Clark died by gunshot wound, John Wesley was shot in the hand, and Murry was shot in the face and almost died. The Falkner family had a history of hard drinking, hard living, economic success, and personal tragedy.

William Cuthbert Faulkner (he added the "u" to his name to accord with that of his earlier ancestors) was born in 1897; his three brothers were born shortly thereafter. Faulkner spent most of his life in and around the small city of Oxford, Mississippi. In his early life, Faulkner was not a success. As a small child, he almost died of scarlet fever, and did not do well in school. Nor was he accepted to fight, as he desired, in World War I; he had to stay home and work odd jobs—as a bookkeeper, as a bookstore assistant, in the University of Mississippi power plant, and then at the post office (from which he was fired).

It looked very much like William Cuthbert Faulkner's life was not going to be very successful. Like his father, Murry, he didn't know quite what to do, and he drank heavily. However, he also had the talents of William Clark and John Wesley; he was destined to live a powerful, if painful, life. William Cuthbert Faulkner took a few college courses and started writing poetry, and his life as a writer was launched when he drifted to New Orleans and met Sherwood Anderson, who helped him to get his first novel published.

From then on, Faulkner knew that he wanted to write, and he tried to make his living that way. Even though this was stressful for him, and he often felt that he had to write for money, he still managed to produce a significant opus of modern literature. His "commercial" writing and his "artistic" writing were not at odds—at first he wrote *Sanctuary* (1931), about a rape, which he hoped would be popular; then he wrote *Absalom, Absalom!* (1936), which he made as difficult as possible. Finally, he combined both styles in his Snopes trilogy—*The Hamlet* (1940), *The Town* (1957), and *The Mansion* (1959)—and the result is a difficult but understandable compendium of Southern style, diction, and poetry. It may be significant that Faulkner's style became clearer as his career progressed.

Despite his successes, William Faulkner led a difficult life. Even though he married his childhood sweetheart, Estelle, she tried to drown herself on their wedding night. Later, they bought "Rowan Oak," a typical antebellum plantation house, dating from 1844. But since his father was not financially solvent, Faulkner felt responsible for his younger brothers as well, so he found himself supporting his establishment and others. He was always working hard to make money. This pressure on him, combined with other things, led to his alcoholism.

According to his biographer, Joseph Blotner, Faulkner drank for a variety of reasons: drinking made him happy, it made him less shy, and it helped him in difficult social situations. Finally, however, he would stop eating and only drink, and then would have delirium tremens for days afterwards. Faulkner also went for long stretches without drinking at all. Once, while working on *Absalom, Absalom!*, Faulkner drank so heavily that he left the manuscript at a hunting cabin 40 miles outside New Orleans. His family often sent him to private sanitariums to recover. However, drunk or sober, he wrote.

Faulkner's reputation continued to grow, but the money he made from his novels was not enough to support his large house, wife, family, and wife's family. Consequently, Faulkner worked, off and on, as a scriptwriter in the Hollywood film industry. This work enabled him to pay his bills. At one point, Faulkner thought that he could sell *Absalom, Absalom!* to the movies.

Faulkner worked on movies or had his own work adapted into Hollywood projects on and off for about 40 years, but he was most active as a scriptwriter from the 1930s through the 1940s.

He began his film career in the 1930s, and among his early efforts were his co-screenwriting credit for *The Road to Glory* (1936), and his credit for contributing dialog to *Slave Ship* (1937).

A few years later, Faulkner was sharing screenwriting credits for what would become two of the finest examples of the film noir genre: *To Have and Have Not* (1944) and *The Big Sleep* (1946). Faulkner's writing helped make these motion pictures—the first based on an Ernest Hemingway novel, the second based on a Raymond Chandler tale—into classics of the American Cinema.

After this high point, Faulkner continued to write movie scripts and to allow some of his novels to be reborn as movies. *The Long*

Hot Summer and *The Tarnished Angels*, both released in 1958, were films based on Faulkner's novels. The following year, his novel, *The Sound and the Fury* also was made into a movie. The film version of *Sanctuary* was released in 1961.

Throughout his life, Faulkner continued having trouble with alcoholism and continued writing—producing books, short stories, screenplays, and poems. As he got older, he began to travel around the world and receive honors, including the Nobel Prize in 1950. When he accepted the Nobel Prize for literature in Stockholm, he said:

> "I feel that this award was not made to me as a man, but to my work—a life's work in the agony and sweat of the human spirit, not for glory and least of all for profit, but to create out of the materials of the human spirit something which did not exist before."

This is certainly an achievement of Faulkner's: whether you like or hate his work, it is clear that what he has done has not been done before. His is an original, clear voice with a special message for the world.

As he grew older, other honors came his way. Faulkner was given an appointment at the University of Virginia, which had a salary but few duties. However, he never wholly left his home of Oxford, Mississippi, and when he died from a heart attack in 1962, he was buried there. Oxford, Mississippi, transformed in Faulkner's fervid imagination to Jefferson, Mississippi, now has an important place in American literary history.

It should be noted that the background of Thomas Sutpen is very similar to William Faulkner's grandfather, William Clark Falkner. The events in the tale—the violence, the manipulations, the murders—are very similar to those in Faulkner's past. At one level, it is his own past that Faulkner is trying to come to terms with, like Quentin, in this novel. As with Quentin in *The Sound and the Fury*, Faulkner was thinking of his own life when he wrote *Absalom, Absalom!* According to Faulkner's biographer, Joseph Blotner, Faulkner always said he wrote from his own experience. Moreover, he told Malcolm Cowley that "I am telling the same story over and over, which is myself and the world."

Historical Background

Absalom, Absalom! was published in 1936, halfway through William Faulkner's long career. The novel is set against the backdrop of the American South from about 30 years before the Civil War, when Mississippi was still wild territory, peopled with Native Americans and hunters, to about 1910. The novel can serve as an illustration of one stage of American history—the settlement of the mid-south just before the Civil War.

Thomas Sutpen's life coincides with the colonilization of the land, which gradually became populated with African slaves, wealthy plantation owners, and poor white sharecroppers. The novel covers the war years, describing what life was like for the women who stayed at home, and the reconstruction, extending until the year 1910. Faulkner's novel *Absalom, Absalom!* chronicles the history of the settlement, slave economy, Civil War, and reconstruction of the American South.

To write *Absalom, Absalom!*, Faulkner created a whole society. He renamed his hometown Jefferson, Mississippi, and called the county Yoknapatawpha; he even drew a map for his readers. Since the plot events in *Absalom, Absalom!* are so deeply buried within the narrative text, Faulkner even provides a chronology. However, *Absalom, Absalom!* is still a difficult novel to read and understand.

Some of the central characters in Faulkner's early novels reappear briefly in *Absalom, Absalom!*, and some introduced in this novel appear later. Faulkner's novels are an ongoing dialogue or narrative, as if several old men were sitting on a porch, telling and re-telling the same old stories. In this way, Faulkner's writing imitates aspects of oral history, one aspect of his Southern heritage. In *Absalom, Absalom!*, Faulkner adds the modern use of stream-of-consciousness narrative to his natural ability to tell stories, and creates a very complicated text.

In *Absalom, Absalom!*, Faulkner used the language of James Joyce and T. S. Eliot—high-modernism—to tell and re-tell the same tale many different ways. The language of modernism, here, is very difficult to understand. *Absalom, Absalom!* requires careful, thoughtful reading, which the first reviewers did not have time to give it. Its first critics called it either boring or disturbing. In fact, when Faulkner sent his publisher the first chapter, the publisher penciled a notation: "This is damned confusing." Still, Faulkner intentionally omitted plot elements in order to make his reader feel as if he or she were one of the storytellers on the porch, and he insisted on publishing *Absalom, Absalom!* in this difficult modernist style.

Fortunately, Faulkner was still working in Hollywood when *Absalom, Absalom!* was published; when the novel failed financially, he still had other income coming in. Although the reviews of 1936 were mixed (Clifton Fadiman, in *The New Yorker*, called it "the most consistently boring novel by a reputable writer to come my way during the last decade"), today *Absalom, Absalom!* is widely accepted as a modernist American classic.

Whatever your opinion, *Absalom, Absalom!* is certainly a dense, interesting, and complicated text, with many layers of meaning, and many levels of understanding. The reader can choose the level at which to enter the novel—as a tale of incest, or as a family history of slavery and murder.

Master List of Characters

Akers—*A poor hunter from Jefferson, who observes the building of Thomas Sutpen's plantation, "Sutpen's Hundred," and reports back to the other townspeople.*

Aunt—*Miss Rosa's and Ellen Coldfield's aunt. Miss Rosa's mother died in childbirth, and her aunt was her only mother-figure. She also planned Ellen's wedding.*

Judge Benbow—*Miss Rosa's lawyer, who helps her out when she is poverty-stricken.*

Eulalia Bon—*Only child of Haitian sugar planter, who married Thomas Sutpen in New Orleans.*

Charles Bon—*Only son of Thomas Sutpen and Eulalia Bon. He becomes engaged to his half-sister Judith, and is murdered by his half-brother Henry.*

Charles Etienne Saint Velery Bon—*Son of Charles Bon and his mistress from New Orleans.*

Jim Bond—*"Idiot" son of Charles Etienne Saint Velery Bon and his African-American wife.*

Clytie (Clytemnestra)—*Daughter of Thomas Sutpen and a slave, who lives in the main house at Sutpen's Hundred.*

Goodhue Coldfield—*Miss Rosa's father, a merchant and town leader.*

Ellen Coldfield—*Goodhue's daughter, who marries Thomas Sutpen; mother of Henry and Judith.*

Miss Rosa Coldfield—*Goodhue's second daughter, to whom Sutpen proposes after Ellen dies. Miss Rosa narrates part of the story.*

General Compson—*Quentin's grandfather, Sutpen's first friend.*

Mr. Compson—*Quentin's father who narrates part of the story.*

Quentin Compson—*A college student at Harvard; although Quentin is marginal to the plot, it is he who is telling the story.*

French Architect—*The architect that Thomas Sutpen brought from Martinique to build his mansion. Sutpen kept him captive on the plantation for two years.*

Haitian Slaves—*Unnamed and unindividualized, Thomas Sutpen's slaves from Haiti nevertheless exist as a major force in* Absalom, Absalom! *Like Sutpen himself, they are a mixture of innocence and savagery, unused to civilized ways.*

Ikkemotubbe—*The Chickasaw Indian agent from whom Thomas Sutpen bought his plantation.*

Melicent Jones—*Wash Jones' daughter.*

Milly Jones—*Wash Jones' granddaughter, seduced by Thomas Sutpen.*

Wash Jones—*Poor white squatter and handyman for Sutpen. Jones kills Sutpen.*

Luster—*Young African-American boy, who is a central character in* The Sound and the Fury.

Major de Spain—*The Jefferson sheriff, who killed Thomas Sutpen's murderer, Wash Jones.*

Shreve McCannon—*Quentin's Canadian roommate at Harvard, to whom Quentin narrates the story.*

Theophilus McCaslin—*One of Faulkner's stock characters, Theophilus McCaslin prayed over Charles Bon's grave while he was being buried.*

Pettibone—*The wealthy plantation owner from whose door Thomas Sutpen was turned away.*

Colonel John Sartoris—*A Faulknerian figure, whom Thomas Sutpen replaced as commanding officer in the Civil War.*

Henry Sutpen—*Son of Thomas and Ellen Sutpen.*

Judith Sutpen—*Daughter of Thomas and Ellen Sutpen.*

Thomas Sutpen—*The upstart patriarch around whom the novel is centered.*

Colonel Willow—*The man who told Thomas Sutpen that his son Henry was wounded.*

Chronology

1807   Thomas Sutpen is born to a large, poor family in West Virginia.

1817   The Sutpen family begins the migration in search of a better life. That same year, Ellen Coldfield is born.

1820   Thomas Sutpen runs away from home to make his fortune in the world.

1827   Thomas Sutpen marries Eulalia Bon, the only child of a French plantation owner, in the West Indies.

1831   Charles Bon, the son of Thomas Sutpen and Eulalia Bon, is born in Haiti. When Thomas Sutpen learns that Eulalia Bon has some African heritage, he abandons his first wife and child.

1833   Thomas Sutpen appears in Jefferson, Mississippi, buys land, and starts to build his plantation, Sutpen's Hundred.

1834   Clytie, the daughter of Thomas Sutpen and a slave, is born.

1835   The mansion at Sutpen's Hundred is almost finished, so Thomas Sutpen allows the French architect to leave and plans to court Ellen Coldfield.

1838   Thomas Sutpen and Ellen Coldfield are married in a ceremony that the townspeople refuse to attend.

1839   Henry Sutpen is born.

1841 Judith Sutpen is born.

1845 Rosa Coldfield is born to middle-aged parents; her mother dies in childbirth.

1850 Wash Jones, a poor white squatter, moves to Jefferson with his daughter Melicent, and camps out on Thomas Sutpen's land.

1853 Milly Jones, daughter of Melicent Jones and granddaughter of Wash Jones, is born.

1859 Henry Sutpen and Charles Bon meet at the University of Mississippi in Oxford; Henry brings Charles home for Christmas; Charles and Judith fall in love; Charles Etienne St. Velery Bon is born in New Orleans.

1860 Henry brings Charles home for Christmas once again; Thomas Sutpen forbids the marriage of Judith and Charles; Henry repudiates his father, leaves with Charles Bon.

1861 Henry Sutpen, Charles Bon, and Thomas Sutpen enlist in the Confederate Army to fight in the Civil War.

1863 Ellen Coldfield Sutpen dies in her darkened room.

1864 Goodhue Coldfield dies of starvation in his attic.

1865 Henry Sutpen and Charles Bon return from the war; Henry shoots Charles at the gate to Sutpen's Hundred. Miss Rosa Coldfield moves out to Sutpen's Hundred to live with Judith Sutpen and Clytie.

1866 Thomas Sutpen returns from the war and proposes to Miss Rosa Coldfield; he suggests that they try to conceive a male child before marriage and she moves back to the town of Jefferson.

1867 Thomas Sutpen begins a relationship with Milly Jones, Wash Jones's granddaughter.

1869 Milly has a daughter by Thomas Sutpen; Wash Jones kills Sutpen, his granddaughter, and her child. Major de Spain, the sheriff of Jefferson, kills Wash Jones.

1870 Charles Etienne St. Velery Bon and his mother, Charles Bon's wife in New Orleans, visit Sutpen's Hundred.

1871   Charles Etienne St. Velery Bon's mother dies in New Or-
        leans, and Clytie travels to New Orleans to bring him back
        to Sutpen's Hundred to live.

1881   Charles Etienne St. Velery Bon brings an African-Ameri-
        can wife to live with him at Sutpen's Hundred.

1882   Jim Bond, developmentally disabled son of Charles
        Etienne St. Velery Bon and his African-American wife, is
        born at Sutpen's Hundred.

1884   Judith Sutpen and Charles Etienne St. Velery Bon die of
        yellow fever.

1909   Miss Rosa and Quentin find Henry Sutpen still living, hid-
        den in the mansion at Sutpen's Hundred; Clytie sets fire
        to the house, killing herself and Henry Sutpen. The only
        known heir to the Sutpen clan is Jim Bond, who escapes
        to the woods.

1910   Quentin Compson recounts this tale to Shreve McCannon
        at Harvard University. Later that year (and in another
        novel), Quentin kills himself.

Summary of the Novel

Absalom, Absalom! is a multi-layered story being told by
Quentin Compson, a young student sitting in his room at Harvard,
to Shreve McCannon, his Canadian roommate. Shreve has asked
Quentin "What is the South like?" In response, Quentin tells him
about Thomas Sutpen, a character based on Faulkner's great-
grandfather, who built a plantation, "Sutpen's Hundred," in the
deep South. The story is told as a series of memories, or gossip
collected from different narrators, some of whom are reliable and
some of whom are not. Although the story is fairly clear-cut, the
layering of the narration makes it seem more of a myth, or mystery, than a history.

Like Faulkner's great-grandfather, William Clark Falkner, Thomas Sutpen is born in West Virginia and runs away at a young age
to make a life for himself. The reason for Sutpen's departure from
his family is that he was ashamed of being the poor, unshod son of
an itinerant alcoholic sharecropper. When he was young, he was
turned away from a plantation door by a liveried slave.

When Sutpen runs away, he goes to the West Indies to make his fortune. He became an overseer on a plantation, and during a rebellion by the slaves, he protected the plantation owner and his daughter. The trauma of the revolution draws the two young people together, and Thomas Sutpen marries Eulalia Bon, the plantation owner's only daughter, thus making his fortune.

When Sutpen returns to the United States, he first lives in New Orleans, where he discovers that Eulalia Bon has some African ancestry. Then he abandons her and their son Charles. Thus, in more ways than one, Thomas Sutpen has made his fortune by using the tools of racism.

Sutpen then makes his way to Mississippi, where he buys a piece of fertile land from the Native Americans. Then, using the labor of slaves imported from Haiti, he carves out a plantation and builds a mansion. Thomas Sutpen has a "grand design" in mind: he wants to become a wealthy plantation owner like the one from whose door he was turned away. In order to gain respectability and a family, he then marries Ellen Coldfield, the daughter of an upright, moral town merchant. Sutpen is arrested just before his wedding (for undisclosed reasons), but Mr. Coldfield bails him out, and the wedding takes place. Nevertheless, none of the townspeople attend the wedding.

Thomas Sutpen nearly accomplishes his grand design. He and Ellen have two children, Henry and Judith, and they live a prosperous life at his mansion on his plantation at Sutpen's Hundred.

Sutpen's past, however, comes back to haunt him. His son from his first marriage to Eulalia Bon, Charles Bon, meets and befriends his son, Henry, at Oxford University. Henry Sutpen does not know that Charles Bon is his half-brother, and he invites Charles home for Christmas. Charles and Judith immediately fall in love. The following Christmas, Charles Bon returns again, and Thomas Sutpen angrily forbids the marriage, telling Henry that Charles is his half-brother. Henry, in return, angrily repudiates his father and runs away with Charles.

The course of these familial events is changed when the Civil War erupts. Henry and Charles (even though he has African blood) enlist on the side of the South, and Thomas Sutpen forms a regiment. The men leave the women to fend for themselves and to try to grow enough food to last through the war years.

When Henry learns that Charles is his half-brother, he is still willing to condone his marriage to Judith, but when, during the war, he learns that Charles has African ancestry, he refuses to condone it. He follows Charles back to Sutpen's Hundred and murders him at the gate, rather than see him marry his sister.

During the Civil War years, Ellen Sutpen dies. After the war, and Henry's murder of Charles, Miss Rosa moves to Sutpen's Hundred. Then Thomas Sutpen returns from the war. Still trying to beget an empire, Thomas Sutpen proposes to Miss Rosa Coldfield. At first, Miss Rosa is happy, but then Sutpen coldly suggests that she try to bear him a son before marriage. Miss Rosa is furious and hates him forever after. Since the main part of the narration of *Absalom, Absalom!* comes from Miss Rosa's knowledge, Thomas Sutpen is most often portrayed as a demon, or devil.

Failing with Miss Rosa, Thomas Sutpen then seduces Wash Jones's granddaughter. Milly Jones becomes pregnant, and when Sutpen goes to the Jones's shack to see if it is a son and thus the heir to his empire, Wash Jones kills him with a scythe. Thomas Sutpen's grand design was also his downfall.

This is the end of the "respectable" Sutpen empire, but Charles Bon is still alive—and he has had a child by a mistress in New Orleans. Clytie the slave is also a daughter of Sutpen's, and brings the younger Charles to Sutpen's Hundred to live. When Charles Etienne grows up, he rebels against the family's racism by marrying a woman of complete African-American ancestry. They, in turn, have an idiot son, Jim Bond, and he is the only survivor of the Sutpen clan.

At the end of the novel, Quentin describes taking Miss Rosa out to the nearly abandoned plantation at Sutpen's Hundred, where they find Henry still alive, but hiding out. When Miss Rosa arrives with an ambulance a few months later, Clytie sees it coming and thinks it is the police, come to arrest Henry Sutpen at last. Consequently, she sets fire to the house, killing herself and Henry. Then the only figure left with Sutpen blood is Jim Bond; Shreve concludes that "I think that in time the Jim Bonds are going to conquer the Western Hemisphere." Jim Bond runs off into the woods, howling, and can be heard from time to time thereafter. Faulkner's message is that the aristocracy of the old South is doomed, due to its own fatal flaws.

Faulkner uses the title *Absalom, Absalom!* to refer to a story in the Old Testament wherein Absalom, the favorite son of King David, rebels against him and is slain by an uncle. The story in the Bible also includes the incest of a brother and sister. This biblical tale is related to the novel: Charles Bon and Judith Sutpen are brother and sister; Henry Sutpen loves Judith Sutpen more than a sister; and Henry, the favorite son, rebels against Thomas Sutpen, the patriarch of the empire.

Estimated Reading Time

Faulkner provides a chronology of events and a genealogy of the characters in *Absalom, Absalom!*, and the reader should consult it every time the novel becomes confusing. Even so, *Absalom, Absalom!* is a very difficult book to read and understand. It is self-consciously written in the style of high-modernism, like James Joyce's *Ulysses* and T. S. Eliot's *The Waste Land,* both first published in 1922. Moreover, some of the narration is through Quentin's eyes, some is through the eyes of his father, and some is through Miss Rosa's eyes. Every major character in the book has a voice through which the tale is told.

Faulkner's prose style is also difficult: he omits punctuation, makes up words, and uses long sentences. Nevertheless, it is fun to read in small portions. By slowly and carefully reading the novel, you can get a sense of the Southern accent and the idiom that he is using. If possible, read a section aloud to get the feel of his language.

Since the style of *Absalom, Absalom!* is a major impediment to understanding and enjoying the novel, these MAXnotes will assist the reader by looking closely at some sections of the text. Faulkner was writing often in "blank verse" so the writing must be seen within the context of poetry. At the same time, the modernism has a self-consciousness about it that refers directly to Faulkner's literary predecessors, such as James Joyce and T. S. Eliot. The reader will be encouraged to take a critical stance regarding Faulkner's use of style—whether you like it or hate it—and therefore enter into a closer understanding of the text.

Reading speed will improve as the reader becomes accustomed to the dense, modernistic style that William Faulkner uses in

Absalom, Absalom! The novel also becomes somewhat more understandable as it progresses, largely due to the reader's increasing knowledge of the plot elements. However, it is a difficult novel, and the reader will have to be prepared to spend some time and effort to understand the style.

In Chapter One, Miss Rosa and Quentin's commentary, is particularly difficult. The reader is suddenly dropped into a story-in-progress, and is expected both to know all the details and to be able to follow Faulkner's long and idiosyncratic sentence structure. However, if the reader persists, the reading should become easier and easier. The estimated reading time for Chapter One is three hours.

Chapters Two and Three are similar to Chapter One, but longer. Consequently, the reading time for each chapter remains three hours.

Chapter Four is a long, difficult, and complex chapter. Consequently, the estimated reading time is five hours. However, Chapters Five and Six are shorter, and begin to give more concrete plot information. Still, given the overall complexity of the material, the reader should allow three hours for each.

Chapter Seven provides a lot of the background information on Thomas Sutpen, and although it is long, it is easier reading than the preceding chapters. Quentin Compson and Shreve McCannon are talking, telling each other the story of the Sutpen dynasty in flashbacks. Since it is the longest chapter in the book, with the most overall information, the reader should pay special attention to it. Estimated reading time is five hours.

Chapter Eight provides more background material, but little that is new. Since it is long, at least four hours should be left to read it. Chapter Nine, the final chapter, is fairly short and provides a good overview of the entire novel. Consequently, it should be read slowly and carefully. Estimated reading time for this chapter is two hours.

The total estimated reading time for *Absalom, Absalom!* is 31 hours.

Absalom, Absalom!

Chapter 1

New Characters:

Miss Rosa Coldfield: *a minor figure in the Sutpen myth; a major narrator in the novel*

Quentin Compson: *the focal narrator of* Absalom, Absalom!

Mr. Compson: *Quentin's father, a major narrator in* Absalom, Absalom!

Thomas Sutpen: *the frontiersman who founded the Sutpen clan; the patriarch around whom the novel is centered*

Summary

The novel *Absalom, Absalom!* begins with a starkly evocative (and typically Faulknerian) scene: Miss Rosa Coldfield, an old Southern lady, and Quentin Compson, a confused young Southerner, are sitting in a dusty, airless, and timeless room, talking. Miss Rosa's legs are so short they barely touch the floor, and Quentin, a college student, does not know why he is there. Nevertheless, the old lady rambles on, telling Quentin the history of the Sutpen clan in the town of Jefferson, Mississippi. Quentin obediently listens to the tale.

Most of the novel is a third or fourth-person account of the events surrounding Thomas Sutpen and his plantation, Sutpen's Hundred. We hear the viewpoints of Miss Rosa, Quentin, Quentin's

father Mr. Compson, and various townspeople as well. From all this evidence, we are left to re-construct the tale as best we can.

Later in *Absalom, Absalom!*, Quentin asks his father why Miss Rosa chose him to tell the tale; Mr. Compson answers that it is because *his* father, Quentin's grandfather General Compson, was the first (and only) man to befriend Thomas Sutpen when he appeared suddenly and unexpectedly in the town of Jefferson. Since that day, the Sutpen family, and thus Miss Rosa's family, has relied on the Compsons as historians and friends.

Miss Rosa talks on and on, seemingly without sense. Her narration is interwoven with Quentin's own thoughts about the subject, and about Miss Rosa herself. Miss Rosa haphazardly tells the story of Sutpen's marriage to her sister Ellen, and their two children, Judith and Henry. Throughout her narrative, Miss Rosa refers to Thomas Sutpen as a "demon" or "ogre" thus displaying her hatred of him.

Miss Rosa hated Thomas Sutpen for a variety of reasons. According to her narration, he "came out of nowhere" and "wasn't even a gentleman," and yet he had the power to build a plantation and to meet and marry her sister. Miss Rosa might have forgiven him for those things, but she would never forgive him for what he did later, when he proposed marriage to her and then added an insulting stipulation.

Thomas and Ellen Sutpen had two children, Judith and Henry, but Sutpen still led a wild, savage life. He invited the town's men to his barn to bet on fights between slaves. He even joined in the fights himself. One night Ellen surprised him in a fight with his three children—Judith, Henry, and Clytie (the daughter of Sutpen and a slave)—watching. Not only was the patriarch fighting a slave, but both were "naked to the waist and gouging at one another's eyes as if their skins should not only have been the same color but should have been covered with fur." According to Miss Rosa, this is the point at which Ellen Sutpen discovers what kind of man she has married—a savage. Chapter One ends with this scene.

Analysis

Some of the main thematic elements of *Absalom, Absalom!* are revealed within the first sentences of the novel. Faulkner's themes of death, the confusion of the past with the present, and the inevitability of history are demonstrated in the very first words that he writes. In the initial image that Faulkner draws of Miss Rosa talking to Quentin, he writes:

> "they sat in what Miss Coldfield still called the office because her father had called it that—a dim hot airless room with the blinds all closed and fastened for forty-three summers because when she was a girl someone had believed that light and moving air carried heat and that dark was always cooler..."

Immediately the reader is told that this is a story made up of other stories: Miss Rosa and Quentin are not only sitting in an office, but what was "still called" an office, since Mr. Coldfield once had called it that. With these few words, we realize that the ghosts of the past will be important throughout the text.

There is also an immediate indication that this is a story made up of myths. For instance, the blinds are shut, not just to keep out the heat, but because *someone once said* that air carried heat. By explaining it in this complex way, Faulkner is suggesting that this is a myth (that air carries heat), and may or may not be true. The same goes for all of the "facts" in this novel: they are recreations of myths told, time and time again, by people long dead or nearing death.

Faulkner also uses many adjectives without connecting commas to stress the mood, as in this description: "a dim hot airless room." This is an example of how he uses language and the tools of poetry to reinforce his theme. If you read "dim, hot, airless room," with correct punctuation, you leave a pause between the adjectives. But, if you read it as Faulkner wrote it—"dim hot airless room"—you end up saying it as if you were breathless, as you would be in such a place. One of the reasons for the great difficulty in reading *Absalom, Absalom!* is that it is in many places a prose poem of magnificent complexity.

That first sentence continues its poetic description of the room:

> "which (as the sun shone fuller and fuller on that side of the house) became latticed with yellow slashes full of dust motes which Quentin thought of as being flecks of the dead old dried paint itself blown inward from the scaling blinds as wind might have blown them..."

Quentin is looking at dust motes as if they were flecks of old paint. Again, we are warned that in this dead, quiet world, reality is in the eyes of the beholder.

Faulkner's dense, modernistic style is immediately evident here. He is influenced by the modernist novelist James Joyce's stream-of-consciousness technique, and by the poetry of T. S. Eliot. Like Joyce and Eliot, Faulkner omits punctuation, uses compound adjectives, makes up words (like "nothusband"), and continually sacrifices clarity to the rhythms and cadences of poetry. Consequently, it is important, especially on a first reading, to read the text closely, out loud if possible. This will make understanding the novel much easier.

Most of the main themes are introduced in the first chapter and the unfolding story gradually takes on a mythic quality. It is a tale remembered in many different ways by different people, the whole of which eventually functions as an analogy of the rise and fall of the American South and the economic system of slavery.

In *Absalom, Absalom!* it is never just Quentin talking, or just the narrator, or Mr. Compson, or Miss Rosa. The entire South speaks through the stories of the characters. The novel is comprised of remembered voices from the past, and these various ghosts who refuse to be silenced. Quentin Compson is merely the "collector" of the parts of the tale, and Miss Rosa's voice, although it is the most persuasive in the novel, is countered by other voices throughout.

Quentin describes his home as "the deep South dead since 1865 and peopled with garrulous outraged baffled ghosts...." It is those garrulous ghosts that Faulkner, through the character Quentin, is trying to come to terms with in the novel *Absalom, Absalom!* Each ghost has a voice in the novel, each ghost has a story to tell, and the final outcome that Quentin discovers is that the economic and social system created by the institution of slavery is unacceptable for human life and fulfillment.

Study Questions

1. Who is the main narrator of *Absalom, Absalom!*?
2. Who is the main character in *Absalom, Absalom!*?
3. How is Miss Rosa related to Thomas Sutpen?
4. Why did Thomas Sutpen marry Ellen Coldfield?
5. How many children does Thomas Sutpen have in Jefferson?

6. Explain the biblical allusion in the title *Absalom, Absalom!*

7. Describe the literary style *Absalom, Absalom!* is written in.

8. What historical event parallels the rise and the fall of the Sutpen dynasty?

9. What historical time-period is Faulkner writing about?

10. What is the name of the town in which Faulkner's story takes place?

Answers

1. Quentin Compson, a young college student, is the narrator.

2. Thomas Sutpen, a frontiersman turned plantation owner, is the main character.

3. Thomas Sutpen married Miss Rosa's older sister, Ellen.

4. Thomas Sutpen married Ellen Coldfield to gain respectability and beget a dynasty.

5. Thomas Sutpen has three children in Jefferson: Henry and Judith, by his wife, and Clytie, by a slave.

6. Absalom is the favorite son of King David who rebels against him and is killed by an uncle.

7. *Absalom, Absalom!* is written in the literary style of high modernism. It breaks many of the standard rules of grammar.

8. The story of the rise and fall of the Sutpen clan parallels the rise and fall of the South.

9. Faulkner is writing about the historical time period from 30 years prior to the Civil War until about 1910 in the American south.

10. *Absalom, Absalom!* is set in Jefferson, Mississippi (based on Oxford, Mississippi), like many of Faulkner's other novels.

Suggested Essay Topics

1. Explain how the biblical allusion in the title of the novel *Absalom, Absalom!* relates to the story.

2. Explore the viewpoint of Miss Rosa's narration. Is she an objective, disinterested narrator, or is she emotionally involved in the story? How would this effect her narration?

3. Write about a story you know, or an incident from your own life using the many-layered, stream-of-consciousness style that Faulkner uses, breaking the standard rules of grammar.

4. Using the information you have learned so far about the Sutpen clan, describe the family's strengths and weaknesses, its failures and accomplishments, and how it triumphs and tragedies were shaped by American history.

Chapter 2

New Characters:

Akers: *a poor Southern hunter who watches the building of Thomas Sutpen's plantation, "Sutpen's Hundred," in the woods. Akers acts as a reporter, telling the other townspeople of Jefferson what is going on*

Aunt: *the "Aunt" referred to is Miss Rosa's and Ellen's aunt. She lived with the Coldfield family, organized Ellen's wedding and, after Miss Rosa's mother died in childbirth, took care of Miss Rosa when she was a child*

Goodhue Coldfield: *Miss Rosa's father, a respectable merchant and town leader*

Ellen Coldfield: *Goodhue's daughter who marries Thomas Sutpen; also the mother of Henry and Judith*

Haitian Slaves: *often called "wild negroes" or "wild niggers," these unnamed slaves from Haiti nevertheless exist as a major force in* Absalom, Absalom! *Like Thomas Sutpen himself, they are newcomers to a savage world*

Ikkemotubbe: *the Chickasaw Indian agent from whom Thomas Sutpen bought the land upon which he built his plantation, "Sutpen's Hundred"*

Summary

   Although Chapter Two is narrated in much the same way as Chapter One, it backtracks in that it gives more details about Thomas Sutpen's arrival in the town of Jefferson, how he built his plantation, and how he became a part of the town.

   According to the Sutpen legend, Thomas Sutpen appeared in Jefferson on a Sunday morning, riding a horse. He bought some land from Ikkemotubbe, a Chickasaw Indian agent, and brought a group of French-speaking slaves and a French-speaking architect to the land to build a plantation. They all lived in the wild while carving out the plantation from the raw land, and the entire town was curious about this man and his enterprise. Where did he come from and why was he doing what he was doing?

   Sutpen never explained anything about himself to the other townspeople—where he came from or where he got his money—because of that they always held him in some distrust. They looked on in amazement as his mansion and estate rose up from the wilds.

   From the first, Thomas Sutpen is characterized as a hard, unscrupulous man. To a certain extent he is a man without a conscience. He bought Haitian slaves to build and work on his plantation, and while they were developing his property, they slept in the mud. He brought an architect from Martinique to design his house. Sutpen kept the architect against his will at the primitive camp, and like the slaves, captured him when he tried to escape. They all lived like this for two years, until the mansion was nearly completed, and Sutpen finally let the architect go.

   As long as Sutpen refused to explain anything about himself to the townspeople, they distrusted him, so he decided to gain respectability in another way. When his plantation and mansion were nearly complete, he began to court Ellen Coldfield, the daughter of the most respected man in town.

   Sutpen had in mind a "grand design" that Faulkner discusses in more detail later: he wanted to be the patriarch of a dependent empire. The motivation for this is hinted at later.

   Thomas Sutpen's marriage to Ellen Coldfield was part of his grand design. Through the marriage, he would become part of the town and gain respectability.

   One of the mysteries in the novel that is never solved is that Sutpen probably entered into an illegal financial arrangement with

Ellen's father, Goodhue Coldfield. This is hinted at in *Absalom, Absalom!* but never fully explained. However, just before the wedding, Thomas Sutpen is arrested, and it is Goodhue who bails him out. Although we never discover the reason for his arrest, it is significant that Mr. Coldfield signed the bond to free him, even though he was an upright, moral man.

In Chapter Two, the wedding of Thomas Sutpen and Ellen Coldfield is described. It is a tragic wedding: even though Ellen invited 100 townspeople, almost no one came. Consequently, she cried throughout the ceremony. When she left the church after the ceremony, a scene symbolic of her future life awaited her. Sutpen's Haitian slaves were holding pine-knot torches in the night, forming a line against the townspeople as they threw garbage and jeered at the couple.

Analysis

The narration in Chapter Two begins from the viewpoint of Quentin and then switches to storytelling by Mr. Compson, Quentin's father. Since Faulkner is an omniscient narrator at the beginning of this chapter, speaking in the third person for Quentin, so it follows that Faulkner's viewpoint is closest to Quentin's in this novel. Faulkner's way of telling and re-telling the story is to gradually add more details and information to its core. In one of the paragraphs where Mr. Compson is speaking, some direct information is given:

> "When they were married, there were just ten people in the church, including the wedding party, of the hundred who had been invited; though when they emerged from the church (it was at night: Sutpen had brought in a half dozen of his wild negroes to wait at the door with burning pine knots) the rest of the hundred were there in the persons of boys and youths and men from the drovers tavern on the edge of town...."

Even though Mr. Compson's narration is not totally reliable (since he heard it from gossip), in excerpts such as this the reader can get a good idea of what the action in the story is. It is scenes such as this—the image of Thomas Sutpen and Ellen Coldfield

Sutpen leaving the church on their wedding night, the latter crying, surrounded by slaves holding torches and the faces of angry
villagers—that probably encouraged Faulkner to try to sell the novel
to Hollywood.

Faulkner's complex manipulation of viewpoint shows how
family myths are made and remade by generations of half-truths.
Eventually, most of the characters have a voice in the novel, and
most of them give their viewpoints. Of course, some of the viewpoints differ, as in real life. The listener, or collector of the tale, like
Quentin, or the reader, can never know the full truth—only the
social web of truths that make up what we call life.

History is formed by a collection of data, of documents referring to a certain period in time. Faulkner is creating history here,
using the most ephemeral of data—the spoken word—and his history, like many histories, has a moral. Faulkner uses the voices of
the ghosts of his past to create a cultural myth, or history, that shows
the inhumanity of the economic system of slavery to be unacceptable. In this sense, *Absalom, Absalom!*, though it may be difficult
to read, provides a good cultural antidote to the romanticism of
slavery in texts such as *Gone With the Wind.*

Study Questions

1. What type of land did Thomas Sutpen buy from
   Ikkemotubbe?

2. Why was Ellen Coldfield crying during her wedding ceremony?

3. In what month and year were Thomas and Ellen Sutpen
   married?

4. Is Thomas Sutpen a moral character?

5. How many years did the French architect work on the mansion at Sutpen's Hundred?

6. Why did the French architect live in a tent and eat venison
   for two years in the wild?

7. The slaves (called "wild negroes") that Thomas Sutpen
   owned came from what country?

8. From what viewpoint is Chapter Two narrated?

9. What happened to Thomas Sutpen just before he got married?

10. Why was Sutpen arrested?

Answers

1. The land that Thomas Sutpen bought from Ikkemotubbe is "a hundred square miles of the best virgin bottom land in the country."

2. Ellen Coldfield was crying because only a few of the 100 guests she had invited attended the wedding.

3. Thomas and Ellen Sutpen were married in June of 1938, five years after Thomas rode into town.

4. Thomas Sutpen is not a moral character because he has no conscience.

5. The French architect worked on the mansion at Sutpen's Hundred for two years.

6. The architect did not leave because Sutpen did not pay him until it was finished.

7. Thomas Sutpen's slaves were from Haiti.

8. Chapter Two is narrated first by an omniscient narrator, then through the eyes of Quentin, and later through the words of Quentin's father, Mr. Compson.

9. Just before he got married, Thomas Sutpen was arrested and thrown in jail, but his future father-in-law bailed him out.

10. It is never told in the novel why Sutpen was arrested.

Suggested Essay Topics

1. Explain how Faulkner's technique of telling and then re-telling the Sutpen story in *Absalom, Absalom!* makes it more realistic as a family myth.

2. Describe the differences and similarities explaining why the slaves that Sutpen owned and the architect he hired were bound to his land. If the slaves fled, what fate would have awaited them? If the architect escaped, what would his fate have been?

3. Sutpen is laying the foundation for the dynasty he dreams of establishing, but we see that its framework is morally rotten. Describe how the brutality underlying Sutpen's dream parallels the slavery economics upon which Southern agriculture depended before the Civil War.

4. Why would an accomplished author such as William Faulkner purposefully leave out an important detail, such as the reason for Sutpen's arrest?

Chapter 3

New Characters:

Charles Bon: *the son of Thomas Sutpen and his first wife, Eulalia Bon, from New Orleans*

Eulalia Bon: *only child of a Haitian sugar planter. Eulalia married Thomas Sutpen, but he repudiated her when he discovered that she had some African ancestry*

Henry Sutpen: *the only son of Thomas and Ellen Sutpen*

Judith Sutpen: *the only daughter of Thomas and Ellen Sutpen*

Clytie: *the daughter of Thomas Sutpen and a slave; Clytie lives in the mansion at Sutpen's Hundred*

Summary

In Chapter Three, the voice is mainly that of Mr. Compson, Quentin's father. He is telling Quentin the story of Miss Rosa's life—how she was born to middle-aged parents years after her sister, Ellen, and how her mother died during childbirth. According to Mr. Compson, Miss Rosa grew up alone with her aunt and father, Goodhue Coldfield, who was a cold and bitter old man.

Goodhue Coldfield was not always a bitter man. Before Thomas Sutpen came to Jefferson, he was an honest and upright Methodist, a man so moral that when he bought slaves he immediately freed them. However, due to his dealings with Sutpen, he is caught in the spider web of the slave economy, and, as he ages, he becomes more and more unhappy.

Mr. Compson further narrates that Mr. Coldfield and Miss Rosa visited Sutpen's Hundred regularly. Although their relations were strained, they made the 12-mile trip twice a year. Then, when the Civil War began, for unknown reasons (likely related to the disgrace of his financial dealings with Thomas Sutpen) Mr. Coldfield nailed himself into the attic, and lived there while Miss Rosa scoured the remains of the family store to survive.

Every day Miss Rosa sent her father food in a basket. Then, one day, the basket didn't come back down. The neighbors broke in and discovered that Goodhue Coldfield had starved himself to death.

The other plot event that is described in this chapter is the first visit of Charles Bon, Thomas Sutpen's first known son, at Christmas. Henry Sutpen had met and befriended Bon at the University of Mississippi in Oxford, without knowing who he was. Bon probably plotted the friendship to gain access to his father. Then, one Christmas, Henry invited Charles Bon home for vacation, and very soon Bon and Judith fell in love.

Charles Bon and Judith Sutpen decided very quickly to get married. Ellen Sutpen and Miss Rosa were delighted with Judith's upcoming wedding; Miss Rosa even stole cloth from her father's store in order to make Judith a trousseau. Thomas Sutpen was quite aware of Charles Bon's heritage, and in later chapters we will see his subsequent actions.

In the meantime, Henry and Judith were very happy because their relationship was closer than usual with brother and sister. As Faulkner describes it, it was "that fierce impersonal rivalry between two cadets in a crack regiment who eat from the same dish and sleep under the same blanket and chance the same destruction and who would risk death for one another not for the other's sake but for the sake of the unbroken front of the regiment itself." Since

Henry was Charles' best friend, he was overjoyed that Charles was marrying his beloved sister.

Ellen Sutpen was the happiest of all and she bloomed while planning this wedding. Faulkner describes her thus:

> "Ellen at the absolute halcyon of her butterfly's summer and now with the added charm of gracious and graceful voluntary surrendering of youth to her blood's and sex's successor, that concurrent attitude and behavior with the engagement's span with which mothers who want to can almost make themselves the brides of their daughters' weddings."

It was as if all of the humiliation that she experienced in her own wedding could be mended by giving a good wedding to her daughter; she lived vicariously through her daughter's happiness. The happiness, however, was not to last, and is foreshadowed by the image at the end of the chapter of a man on a mule desperately calling at Miss Rosa's gate.

Analysis

Mr. Compson is still telling the story to Quentin in Chapter Three. However, since he is now relaying information third hand—what the others told Miss Rosa and what Miss Rosa told him—it is doubly suspect. Some of the facts that Mr. Compson presents are inaccurate, and others are just omitted.

The narrative style of *Absalom, Absalom!* manages to tell a dramatic story in colloquial Southern language and in a modernist style without sacrificing too much suspense. Even though it is sometimes hard to read, Faulkner presents the events thoroughly (if sometimes inaccurately), one at a time, and the reader can gradually get the whole dramatic picture.

Nevertheless, the novel is still a difficult one to read. It requires a real commitment on the part of the reader. If the reader persists, eventually the reader becomes a *part* of the tale. One of Faulkner's techniques of narration is to refer to events as if the reader already knows the background—as if he, the narrator, is continuing a conversation with the reader begun a long time ago. Consequently, he

casts backwards and forwards in time within each paragraph, and sometimes even within a sentence. Thus, even though the main action of Chapter Three is Mr. Compson's narration to Quentin about Miss Rosa's life, the action of Chapter Four is already being foreshadowed in passages such as this:

> "But anyway, when Christmas day came, Henry and Bon were gone. And Ellen was not visible (she seemed to have retired to the darkened room which she was not to quit until she died two years later) and nobody could have told from either Sutpen's or Judith's faces or actions or behavior, and so the tale came through the negroes: of how on the night before Christmas there had been a quarrel between, not Bon and Henry or Bon and Sutpen, but between the son and the father and that Henry had formally abjured his father and renounced his birthright and the roof under which he had been born and that he and Bon had ridden away in the night...."

Here Faulkner stops mid-story to tell us that Henry and Charles Bon are going to disappear, Ellen Sutpen is going to die, and Henry and his father are going to fight; he tells us this as if we already knew it, as if it were in our minds, as well as his. This technique not only involves the reader in the tale, but it also implicates the reader, by assuming the reader is at one with Faulkner's mind.

By the method of foreshadowing demonstrated above, Faulkner keeps the story going and the reader reading. Faulkner was a master of the modernist mode of expression, but he was also a good craftsman, using drama, romance, violence, and suspense in order to lure the reader into his tale, and keep the reader there until the end. In some of his novels, such as *Sanctuary* (1931), in which a woman gets raped by a man holding a corn-cob, Faulkner used more lurid material to gain a readership. Faulkner used every technique available in modern literature to tell his tale.

Study Questions

1. What was the final result of Sutpen's dealings and interaction with Mr. Coldfield?

2. How did Miss Rosa take care of her father during the Civil War?

3. How did Miss Rosa discover that Mr. Coldfield had died?

4. Who sewed Judith's trousseau?

5. Where was the material for the trousseau from?

6. Did Ellen Sutpen approve of Judith's betrothal?

7. What insect does Ellen Sutpen resemble?

8. Who narrates Chapter Three?

9. Why is the narration in Chapter Three suspect in authenticity?

10. How is the future foreshadowed at the end of this chapter?

Answers

1. The end result of the interaction between Thomas Sutpen and Mr. Coldfield was that Mr. Coldfield shut himself in the attic for an unknown reason.

2. Miss Rosa fed her father during the Civil War years by taking food from their closed grocery store and placing it in a basket which he then pulled up through a window in the attic.

3. "One morning the hand did not come out to draw up the basket". The neighbors broke in and found three days' uneaten food by his bed.

4. Miss Rosa sewed the trousseau.

5. Miss Rosa stole the linen from her father's store to sew the trousseau.

6. Ellen Sutpen is very happy about her daughter's wedding.

7. Ellen Sutpen is likened to a butterfly at the "absolute halcyon" of her summer.

8. Chapter Three is a recounting of a conversation between Mr. Compson and Quentin, in which Mr. Compson relays the information that Miss Rosa told him.

9. Miss Rosa's narration is suspect because she is an embittered old woman who hates Thomas Sutpen and therefore Mr. Compson's narration is suspect.

10. The future is foreshadowed by a voice at the end of the chapter calling for "Rosie Coldfield."

Suggested Essay Topics

1. Describe what happened to Mr. Coldfield and why, if he was a good man before he became wrapped up in Sutpen's world, why was the good man changed and destroyed by his dealings with the evil man? How would it have been if things had worked out the other way around—if the evil man had been changed by the good man?

2. Follow the transformation of Ellen Sutpen as outlined in this chapter. Why is it tragic?

3. Much of the happiness that people experience in this section will turn out to be ephemeral. Write an essay describing the time shifts and foreshadowings that illuminate what you know so far about the past, the present, and the future of one of Faulkner's people.

4. Describe Faulkner's various narrative techniques that he uses in *Absalom, Absalom!* and their effect on the reader.

Chapter 4

New Character:

Wash Jones: *the poor white squatter who comes to Jefferson after Miss Rosa is born and lives at Sutpen's Hundred*

Summary

At the beginning of each chapter, Faulkner brings us back to the beginning of the novel by portraying Quentin as sitting with

Miss Rosa, listening to her stories or waiting to drive her out to Sutpen's Hundred. Then the other voices join in. In Chapter Four, Mr. Compson's voice is very much present in Quentin's head, as Quentin remembers when Mr. Compson showed him a letter.

The main story in this section is about the relationship among the three children of Thomas Sutpen—Henry Sutpen, Judith Sutpen, and Charles Bon. After Henry brought Charles home with him that Christmas, Charles and Judith fell in love. Judith and Henry already loved each other. Since Henry met Charles at college, Henry loved Charles. When Judith loved Charles the circle became complete. This is the section from which the novel takes its title, *Absalom, Absalom!* (referring to the biblical story of incest), and it is one of the longest in the book.

Henry and Charles are nearly as "in love" as Charles and Judith; Mr. Compson also thinks Judith and Henry are closer than is appropriate for siblings. Chapter Four is mainly about Henry's relationship with Charles, than the impending marriage to Judith. Faulkner needs to explain the motivation for the action of the characters and the ensuing catastrophe.

When Thomas Sutpen learns of the marriage plans between Judith and Charles, he tells Henry that Charles Bon is also his son. Although Henry is shocked that Charles would deceive him in order to befriend him and make his way into the family, he remains constant in his affection for Charles. He and Charles leave together, enlisting in the Civil War. Faulkner puts these words in quotations, emanating from Mr. Compson's mouth:

> "Because Henry loved Bon. He repudiated blood birthright and material security for his sake, for the sake of this man who was at least an intending bigamist even if not an out and out blackguard, and on whose dead body four years later Judith was to find the photograph of the other woman and child."

This is an example of how Faulkner gives the reader a plot clue that may be overlooked on a first reading. This is the only mention in *Absalom, Absalom!* of the photograph of Charles Bon's wife and child in New Orleans.

The revelation that Charles Bon is part African-American is a shock for the entire family. Henry and Judith's mother, Ellen, retire to a darkened room, where she lives for two years while she (in typical Faulknerian manner) wastes away and dies. But like Henry, Judith remains steadfast in her love for Charles, and she waits to hear from him.

The letter that Mr. Compson is in the process of showing Quentin is from Charles to Judith (Judith had given it to Mr. Compson's mother to keep). In that letter, Charles describes the difficulty of fighting in the Civil War. He tells Judith to wait for him. Consequently, Judith spends the war years alone, trying to grow enough food to eat, and stitching clothes from rags. Judith saved the scraps of good material from which to sew her wedding dress.

During the war years, the women were reduced to the basic elements of life: seeking food, shelter, and clothing. They lived together at Sutpen's Hundred without the men—Thomas Sutpen had also enlisted in the war, as a colonel. Judith remained steadfast in her commitment to Charles.

During the war, Charles was decorated by the Confederates for bravery. This is ironic in view of later events, when it is revealed that he is part African himself. During the war, Henry also learned that not only was Charles his half-brother, but he was one-sixteenth African-American as well. Henry vowed never to let the marriage happen. This is another example of the moral bankruptcy inherent in racism: Henry condoned the marriage when he knew it was incest, but he condemned it when he learned that it was miscegenation.

When the war was over, the men began to straggle home. Charles set off to Sutpen's Hundred to meet and marry Judith, as he had promised, and Henry set off after him. Just as Charles finally approached the gate to Sutpen's Hundred, Henry caught up with him and shot him rather than see him marry his sister.

The final image in this chapter is of the poor white squatter, Wash Jones, shouting for Miss Rosa to come because there had been a tragedy in her family.

Analysis

In *Absalom, Absalom!,* all the characters' voices are recalled in a stylized, modernist manner, so that sometimes they all sound alike. As Joseph Blotner writes in his biography of Faulkner, as the novel continues, even Shreve's "normally colloquial Canadian" voice becomes Hellenized, like Mr. Compson's voice, and full of high-flown rhetoric, like Miss Rosa's voice. Thus, Shreve sees Sutpen in relation to Miss Rosa as "a widowed Agamemnon to her Cassandra an ancient still-jointed Pyramus to her eager though untried Thisbe...." It is sometimes difficult to tell where one character's thoughts end and another's begin.

Moreover, Faulkner writes as if the reader already knew everything. Faulkner's difficult style forces the reader to identify with the town of Jefferson and even the Sutpen clan. Since we have to trust our instincts and partially reconstruct the story ourselves, as if we were family, which makes the story more intimate. *Absalom, Absalom!* is constructed like a family saga, made not of written narrative fiction, but crafted from spoken gossip. However, the modernist style is very difficult to read, and the reader may want to cover only short sections, one at a time.

The more modernist, abstract sections of *Absalom, Absalom!* alternate with other sections where the narrative voice is clear, hard, and dramatic. For instance, in the description of Henry and Charles in front of the gate to Sutpen's Hundred, Faulkner uses concrete adjectives and images to show, in detail, two men coming home from war:

> "They faced one another on the two gaunt horses, two men, young, not yet in the world, not yet breathed over long enough to be old but with old eyes, with unkempt hair and faces gaunt and weathered as if cast by some spartan and even niggard hand from bronze, in worn and patched gray weathered now to the color of dead leaves, the one with the tarnished braid of an officer, the other plain of cuff, the pistol lying yet across the saddle bow unaimed, the two faces calm, the voices not even raised..."

Then, switching to italics to denote conversation, Faulkner gives a few words of simple spoken language to complete the dramatic moment: *"Dont you pass the shadow of this post, this branch, Charles;* and *I am going to pass it, Henry."* Faulkner ends the chapter with the more colloquial language of the poor white squatter,

Wash Jones, as he shouts to Miss Rosa "Air you Rosie Coldfield? Then you better come on out yon. Henry has done shot that durn French feller. Kilt him dead as a beef." This is an example of how Faulkner's poetic language comes together with direct, dramatic rendition of colloquial language to create a strong and exciting form of prose.

In *Absalom, Absalom!* Faulkner is using an experimental technique of mixing poetic prose and Greek and modernist influences with the directness of colloquial language. In his later novels, he comes to rely more and more on standard, spoken English. This novel shows the possibilities that are created when an author sees no limits on the use of language; the shifting of perspectives, of time, past and present, of voice, of language all result in a compound musical construction that can be "heard" as much as read. It is still left to the reader, though, to orchestrate the construction in his or her mind. Since the shifts are so subtle and frequent in this novel, this is a difficult task indeed.

The result of Faulkner's technique, however, is that meaning is carried in the sound of the language as well as in the content of the words themselves. This is one of Faulkner's great strengths.

Study Questions

1. How does Henry feel about Charles Bon when he first brings him home?

2. Who is more sophisticated, Henry Sutpen or Charles Bon?

3. Why do Henry and Charles leave Jefferson suddenly?

4. What does Ellen do after Henry and Charles leave?

5. Who is the letter from that Mr. Compson is showing Quentin?

6. Who is the letter to?

7. What is the letter about?

8. Who brought the news of the murder to Miss Rosa?

9. What is a good way to read and understand this novel?

10. What is the name of the literary style in which *Absalom, Absalom!* was written?

Answers

1. When Henry Sutpen first brings Charles Bon home at Christmas vacation, they are the best of friends.

2. Charles Bon, from New Orleans, is more sophisticated. Henry Sutpen, who never before left Jefferson, is provincial in clothes, manner, and speech.

3. Henry and Charles leave Jefferson suddenly because Thomas Sutpen has confessed that Charles is his son and can therefore not marry Judith. In their anger, they join the Civil War.

4. After Henry and Charles leave Sutpen's Hundred, Ellen Sutpen retires to a dark room, in which she eventually dies.

5. The letter that Mr. Compson is showing Quentin is from Charles Bon.

6. The letter is to Judith Sutpen.

7. The letter describes the Civil War and tells Judith that he does not know when he will return, but that he will return to marry her.

8. Wash Jones, Sutpen's handyman, brought the news of Charles Bon's murder by his half-brother, Henry, to Miss Rosa Coldfield.

9. A good way to read this chapter is in small pieces; the best way to understand it is to read it several times.

10. The name of the literary style in which *Absalom, Absalom!* was written is "modernism."

Suggested Essay Topics

1. Racism effects the people who perpetuate it as well as the people against whom it is perpetuated. Describe the various ways in which the book shows racism destroying the lives of the major and minor characters.

2. Having more that one family on more than one side of the so-called color line was not unheard of in the days before the Civil War. Write an essay using the novel and at least one

other historical source to describe the social conditions that made such double, secret lives possible.

3. Create your own hypothesis as to why Faulkner would use an unreliable narrator and an incomplete story. What does he achieve by writing in this manner? What does he lose?

4. Describe the emotional and familial relationships between Henry, Judith, and Charles. How are they close? How are they distant? How does this effect the action of *Absalom, Absalom!*?

Chapter 5

New Character:

Theophilus McCaslin: *present during the burial of Charles Bon, he said a Confederate prayer over the Catholic man*

Summary

Chapter Five is the end segment of Miss Rosa's story. It tells the events of the Sutpen drama as they related to her, and then her voice is left behind.

The plot is simple. After Wash Jones brings the news to Miss Rosa of Charles Bon's murder, Miss Rosa immediately goes out to Sutpen's Hundred. Miss Rosa, Judith, Clytie, and Theophilus McCaslin are the only ones who were present at Charles Bon's funeral. They carry the coffin, dig the grave, and bury Charles Bon together.

After the burial, Miss Rosa decides to stay on at Sutpen's Hundred. There, the three women live "the busy eventless lives of three nuns in a barren and poverty-stricken convent," trying to grow enough food to eat. Miss Rosa no longer has a place in town after her father's death: the store was ruined, and she needed food, shelter, and company. Consequently, she plans to honor her sister Ellen's last wishes, and "take care" of her niece Judith.

Miss Rosa lived at Sutpen's Hundred for seven months, until Thomas Sutpen straggled home from the war. Although they occupy the house together, the women rarely see Thomas Sutpen, except at mealtime: they inhabit the inner world of the house, and he inhabits the outdoors.

However, three months later, Thomas Sutpen unexpectedly proposes marriage to Miss Rosa. His way of doing it is typically blunt—he walks into Judith's bedroom, where the three women sit each evening, puts his hand on Miss Rosa's head and says: "You may think I made your sister Ellen no very good husband.... I believe I can promise that I shall do no worse at least for you."

At first Miss Rosa was happy to be engaged. She was still young and had no other prospects. However, Thomas Sutpen then suggests that they attempt to conceive a son before marriage, and Miss Rosa is horrified at his callousness. She returns to Jefferson to live the life of a poor spinster and bears him a grudge for the rest of her life.

This chapter ends with a flashback to the scene in which Henry rushes into Judith's bedroom and tells Judith that he has just shot and killed her fiancé, Charles. Faulkner now gives us the dialogue that ensued between Henry and Judith. Like that between Henry and Charles (just before Henry shot Charles), it is very simple and direct:

> Now you cant marry him.
> Why cant I marry him?
> Because he's dead.
> Dead?
> Yes. I killed him.

After giving the reader this brief but important piece of dialogue, Faulkner reveals something else to carry the readers interest—a suspenseful element.

At the end of the chapter, Faulkner finally tells us why Miss Rosa has called Quentin to her house. Miss Rosa tells Quentin that there is still "something" at Sutpen's Hundred, something "living hidden in that house." Miss Rosa has asked Quentin to go with her and see what or who it is.

Analysis

Faulkner's use of extremely simple, direct dialogue functions well as a contrast to his more florid, poetic language. As in Chapter Four, in Chapter Five, Faulkner creates a contrast at a structurally significant moment—in this case, at the end of the chapter, at a point where the author wants to create dramatic suspense to keep the reader reading.

Faulkner stresses the suspense by giving us only partial information about what might be in the house. It is a hint, to keep us reading, that something dramatic is about to happen. In terms of literary style, it is a bone—the mystery of the "something" in the house—to keep us worrying at his text. At this point, we cannot tell whether it is a natural or supernatural being, and the reader is naturally curious.

Chapter Five is written almost entirely in italics. The use of italics signifies a shift to a different depth of language. It is no longer Mr. Compson telling Quentin stories. It is Miss Rosa speaking for herself again, but at a different level, as if the story had become separated from the participants and had entered the realm of universal myth. The story, which is mainly about a man, Thomas Sutpen, is told mainly by a woman—Miss Rosa; in many cultures it is the women who are the bearers of the tales.

The final section, the recapitulation of the murder of Charles Bon, is not written in italics, and that signifies that this is a pivotal scene in the novel. It is told in direct, dramatic speech, from the viewpoint of the omniscient narrator, the voice that sees all. It is as if Faulkner were taking the reader through stages, as in a film, first giving us soft focus and showing us blaring newspaper headlines.

Study Questions

1. How far is Sutpen's Hundred from the town of Jefferson?
2. What happened to Ellen Sutpen during the Civil War?
3. What happened to Ellen Sutpen's flower beds during the Civil War?
4. Why does Miss Rosa choose to live at Sutpen's Hundred?
5. Who else is living at Sutpen's Hundred?
6. Why does Thomas Sutpen propose marriage to Miss Rosa?

7. Why does Miss Rosa refuse him?

8. From what cloth did Judith sew her wedding dress?

9. What is the purpose of the use of italics in this chapter?

10. Who is the main narrator of Chapter Five?

Answers

1. Thomas Sutpen's plantation, Sutpen's Hundred, is located 12 miles from the town of Jefferson.

2. Ellen Sutpen retired to her room after learning that Charles Bon was her husband's son, and gradually faded away until she died in her darkened bedroom.

3. Ellen Sutpen's flower gardens became ruined and weed-choked.

4. Miss Rosa chooses to live at Sutpen's Hundred for the basic necessities of life: food, shelter, and company. Also, she was asked by Ellen Sutpen, on her deathbed, to take care of her niece Judith.

5. Judith Sutpen and Clytie are also living at Sutpen's Hundred with Miss Rosa.

6. Thomas Sutpen wants to continue building a patriarchy, and sees Miss Rosa as a possible wife who could bear him children.

7. She refuses him because Thomas Sutpen proposed that he and Miss Rosa try to conceive a male child before marriage.

8. Judith sewed her wedding dress from stolen scraps of satin and lace.

9. Italics are used in order to denote a new shift in the depth of the tale: they denote that we are now getting Miss Rosa's own words, not Quentin's memory of them, as in previous chapters.

10. Miss Rosa is the main narrator of Chapter Five.

Suggested Essay Topics

1. Discuss the changing relationship of Miss Rosa with Thomas Sutpen. What did she do after he made his second proposal, and why? Is she a reliable narrator or not?

2. Describe the sudden change, at the end of the chapter, from Miss Rosa's first-person italicized stream-of-consciousness to Faulkner's omniscient voice. How does it heighten the suspense?

3. Strength and weakness are two great themes of this novel, from characters who starve themselves to death, to men who march off to war to escape trouble at home. Using this section of the book, describe examples of strength and weakness displayed by two of the characters.

4. In this novel, where soldiers go off to war while women stay home and make do with almost nothing, sex roles shape people's lives very strongly. Write an essay describing the ways in which the novel's men and women transcend and are limited by their sex-defined roles.

Chapter 6

New Characters:

Judge Benbow: *Miss Rosa's lawyer, who helps her when she is poverty-stricken*

Charles Etienne Saint Velery Bon: *son of Charles Bon and his mistress from New Orleans*

Shreve McCannon: *Quentin's Harvard roommate, with whom he is narrating the story*

Luster: *an African-American boy who is a major character in Faulkner's novel* The Sound and the Fury

Summary

Using a technique seen in the earlier chapters, the beginning of Chapter Six recalls the reader to the "present," only in this case the "present" has changed and now we must change our perceptions with it. We are no longer sitting with Quentin and Miss Rosa, waiting to go out and see what is at Sutpen's Hundred; we are recalling the entire story from the safe distance of Quentin's dormitory room at Harvard University, far away in the north.

Suddenly, the reader is required to shift the whole focus of the narrative framework. The time is now 1910, and two students are sitting, in the night, recalling the myth of the Sutpen clan. From now on, the reader is to understand that the narrative is a story being told by two young men, Quentin Compson and his Canadian roommate, Shreve McCannon.

The chapter begins with an image of snow on Shreve's sleeve, thereby bringing us into a concrete present. The small detail of winter weather reminds us that we are listening to two young men up North at Harvard University. Then Quentin produces a letter from his father announcing Miss Rosa's death. This letter may have precipitated the tale, or maybe Quentin brought it out to illustrate the tale; we never know. However, from now on, part of the method of narration of the tale is a dialogue between these two young men.

Quentin talks, then Shreve talks. Shreve adds a lively voice of modern disbelief to the gothic Southern story especially in statements such as "this old dame grew up in a household like an overpopulated museum." Since Shreve, like the reader, is trying to put together the pieces and understand the tale; he reiterates parts of it to make sure he's clear, and Quentin answers "yes."

At one point while Shreve is talking, Quentin suddenly realizes that Shreve reminds him of his father. Then an italicized flashback begins, in which Quentin remembers that he and his father went to the graveyard to see the graves of the Sutpens and Coldfields.

Thomas Sutpen paid for his grave and that of his wife, but even in death he did not divulge his place or date of birth. Miss Rosa bought the other graves with money she got from her father's store; one by one the family buried each other, making (or borrowing) just enough money for the headstones.

Finally Quentin remembers the story of Charles Etienne Saint Velery Bon. He was the child of Charles Bon, born the same year that Charles met Henry in college. Charles Etienne St. Velery Bon

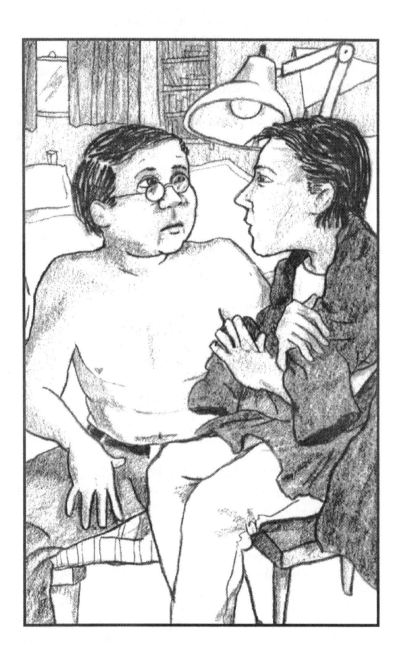

and his unnamed mother went to visit Sutpen's Hundred after Thomas Sutpen was killed. Later, when he was orphaned in New Orleans, Judith sent Clytie to fetch him, and brought him there to live.

During this section, Faulkner gives us his view of women. It is while Mr. Compson is talking again to Quentin, and Quentin is remembering, that the author writes:

> "They lead beautiful lives—women. Lives not only divorced from, but irrevocably excommunicated from, all reality. That's why although their deaths, the instant of dissolution, are of no importance to them since they have a courage and fortitude in the face of pain and annihilation which would make the most spartan man resemble a puling boy, yet to them their funerals and graves, the little puny affirmations of spurious immortality set above their slumber, are of incalculable importance."

This theme has been constant throughout this novel, and it reappears in Faulkner's other novels. Faulkner sees women as super-human, tied more strongly to nature than men, and therefore as being somehow more savage than men.

Race is also an important issue in this chapter. When Charles Etienne St. Velery Bon moves to Sutpen's Hundred, he first slept on a trundle bed between the full bed of his aunt, Judith, and the floor pallet of his other aunt, Clytie. From the first, Clytie will not allow the boy to play with African-American children, so he spends most of his time alone. When Charles Etienne St. Velery Bon becomes a teenager, he moved his sleeping place to the hall, and Clytie moved with him. Later, he made a room for himself in the attic.

Charles Etienne St. Velery Bon grew up angry and confused. Finally he solved his problem by marrying a black woman [with] an authentic wedding license. However, this shocked the townspeople of Jefferson and the South, so that Charles Etienne St. Velery Bon was always getting into fights. He flaunted his marriage continuously, and this caused him to be beaten often. He was also a gambler, so he led a difficult and violent life. Finally, he died of yellow fever. Judith died attending him.

Miss Rosa enlisted the help of Judge Benbow, her lawyer, to buy and inscribe a headstone for Judith. It said that Judith "Suffered the Indignities and Travails of this World for 42 Years, 4 Months, 9 Days, and went to Rest at Last," ending with the words: "Pause, Mortal; Remember Vanity and Folly and Beware."

Luster, an African-American boy who is a major character in *The Sound and the Fury*, has a brief say as Quentin remembers his father recalling Luster's fear in the face of the Sutpen curse. Caught in a sudden rain, Luster won't go into the mansion at Sutpen's Hundred because he is afraid of Jim Bond, the disabled son of Charles Etienne St. Velery Bon and his unnamed wife.

Analysis

Chapter Six begins with some of the techniques used in Chapter Four. It attempts to bring the reader back into a "present"; however, this present is a different present than we thought at the beginning of the novel. It is now clear that the outer framework of *Absalom, Absalom!* is a conversation, or ongoing dialogue, taking place between two young men. Their series of variously formed recollections are being revealed in a dormitory room at Harvard University in 1910.

However, the style soon becomes just as strange and modernistic as in the preceding chapters. It is Shreve who is narrating the story now, and Quentin is listening and saying "yes." It becomes a point-counterpoint recitation of musicality, where Shreve is unwinding the tale and Quentin is punctuating it with the comment "yes." In this sense, it is also like a court addressing a witness. Even just a quick look at the structure of the chapter reveals that it consists of long, loquacious diatribes given on the topic of the Sutpen clan by Shreve, punctuated by comments from Quentin. One paragraph ends and another begins in this manner:

> "'and then almost before his foot was out of the stirrup he (the demon) set out and got himself engaged again in order to replace that progeny the hopes of which he had himself destroyed?'
> 'Yes,' Quentin said.

'Came back home and found his chances of descendants gone where his children had attended to that, and his plantation ruined, fields fallow except for a fine stand of weeds . . ."

Even though Shreve's diction and rhetoric is strange and changeable, and even though the verbal exchange between the two young men is stylized, Shreve does go over all the material fairly systematically, as if he were reviewing a text. In this chapter the reader can catch up with any lost facts.

However, just in case the reader is feeling too secure, Faulkner suddenly introduces Luster, a character from a different novel, to illustrate the strangeness of the inhabitants at Sutpen's Hundred. This sudden introduction of a new character, who then disappears, unsettles the reader yet again.

Still, bit by bit the pieces of the story are coming together: we now know the history of Ellen Coldfield and Miss Rosa; the ensuing events of the Civil War years, including the murder of Charles Bon; and the history of Charles' son, Charles Etienne St. Velery Bon.

Faulkner has also outlined his major themes—a confusion of the past with the present; a confusion of social caste and race; and the blurred lines of proposed familial incest. The confusion of the past and present and the theme of incest are even more central to Faulkner's equally difficult *The Sound and the Fury*. It is the question of race that is most important in this novel.

The only major plot element that we have yet to understand is the moral make-up of Thomas Sutpen, why he started this "empire" in the way he did, and what led to his success, and his ruin.

Absalom, Absalom! is, at one level, a novel about morality. The Sutpen Empire is built on the various sins of greed, callousness to human suffering, indifference, anger, and the cold manipulation of human lives. The empire grows, and is rich, but then it causes its own decline. The very foundation upon which it rested was throughly corrupt.

Study Questions

1. Who are the main narrators of this chapter?
2. What is their verbal relationship?

3. How does Faulkner bring the reader's perceptions and expectations back into a "present"?

4. What is the letter that Quentin is holding in his hand about?

5. Which character freely uses colloquial language like "this old gal" and "this old dame"?

6. Who does Quentin think Shreve sounds like?

7. What scene does Quentin remember?

8. Which character is often referred to as "the demon"?

9. Who does the demon drink moonshine with while laying on a hammock?

10. How is Charles Etienne Bon related to Judith and to Clytie?

Answers

1. Quentin Compson and Shreve McCannon, two students at Harvard, are the two main narrators of this chapter.

2. Shreve is telling the story as a series of questions directed at Quentin, and Quentin is answering "yes."

3. When Faulkner wants to shift the time setting of the narrative to the present, he provides some concrete details, such as dust on the blinds or snow on a sleeve.

4. The letter that Quentin is holding is a letter from his father, announcing the death of Miss Rosa.

5. Shreve McCannon uses colloquial language like "this old gal" and "this old dame."

6. Quentin thinks Shreve sounds like his father, Mr. Compson.

7. Quentin remembers when he and his father visited the graveyard to see the headstones of the Sutpen and Coldfield clans.

8. Thomas Sutpen is often referred to as "the demon" by Miss Rosa, and by others who have heard her tale.

9. Thomas Sutpen, the demon, drinks moonshine while laying on a hammock with Wash Jones, the itinerant handyman.

10. Charles Etienne Bon is a nephew to both Judith Sutpen and Clytie.

Suggested Essay Topics

1. Describe the relationship between Charles Etienne, Judith, and Clytie. How are they alike? How are they dissimilar?

2. Why would Faulkner anchor his story in the "most recent present" of a room at Harvard in which two students are having a discussion?

3. Using examples from this section of the book, describe and discuss how Faulkner portrays women. How does he say they are similar or different from men?

4. This book is very much a story about the bonds of kinship and friendship. Using examples from the book, compare and contrast the obligations and responsibilities of kinship and friendship. Which relationships are more important? Which relationships are honored or violated most often in this book?

Chapter 7

New Characters:

French Architect: *Thomas Sutpen brought him from Martinique to build his mansion and kept him captive on the plantation for two years, until the house was nearly finished*

General Compson: *Quentin Compson's grandfather, Mr. Compson's father, Thomas Sutpen's first (and only) friend*

Melicent Jones: *Wash Jones' daughter, who gives birth to Milly Jones in 1853*

Milly Jones: *Wash Jones' granddaughter, seduced by Thomas Sutpen, who gives birth to a baby girl and is killed, with her baby, by her father, Wash Jones*

Major de Spain: *the Jefferson sheriff who killed Wash Jones*

Pettibone: *the wealthy plantation owner from whose door Thomas Sutpen was turned away, during an incident that inspired Sutpen to build his own empire*

Summary

In Chapter Seven, Faulkner finally gives us the motivation for Thomas Sutpen's seemingly inhuman actions. The story came originally from Sutpen himself, in strange circumstances. The French architect, who Sutpen forced to live in a tent for two years, has escaped, so Sutpen is pursuing him with his slaves and dogs, and General Compson is along for the ride. When the architect tricks them by using engineering skills to propel himself a long distance, the slaves and the dogs lose his scent. While waiting for them to find it again, Sutpen recounts the story of his boyhood to General Compson

Thomas Sutpen came from an impoverished family in the West Virginia mountains. When he was young, his family set off to make a better living, but his mother, who provided the main impetus for the trip and for the family's stability, died on the way. Sutpen's father was an alcoholic who was barely able to keep the family on the road. He kept stopping at taverns, drinking, and losing all the money the family had.

Eventually, as Faulkner writes: "taverns now become hamlets, hamlets now become villages, villages now towns and the country flattened out now with good roads and fields and niggers working in the fields while white men sat fine horses and watched them…" The Sutpen family found a place to live and settled down once again, on the Pettibone plantation.

The Sutpens became sharecroppers and there Thomas Sutpen learned the cruel lesson of social division. One day he went to deliver a message to the plantation house, but was turned away from the front door by a well-dressed African-American slave. He never forgot this humiliation. The rest of the Sutpen myth, and Sutpen's "grand design" to build a plantation and be a patriarch himself, is an attempt to overcome this humiliation.

During his school years, Thomas Sutpen decided he would rather be a slave owner than be a slave. In school, he learned that people "made their fortunes" in the West Indies, so he took his chances and sailed there, where he defended a French plantation against a Haitian uprising. In doing so, he met and married the plantation owner's daughter who, in a plot complication, both made him wealthy and provoked a dilemma. He discovered that she was part African herself, which meant that she could not help him to further his grand design of creating a racist economic system. Sutpen repudiated Eulalia Bon and divorced her, leaving her and their son in New Orleans. Sutpen himself moved on to Jefferson, Mississippi.

The chapter ends with the final tragic event in Sutpen's life. After Miss Rosa refuses his proposition to try to have a son, Sutpen seduces Milly Jones, the granddaughter of his handyman, Wash Jones. When she gives birth, Sutpen rides to her shack to see if it is a male. Jones kills Sutpen with a scythe, and kills his granddaughter and the child as well.

In an ironic tragedy, the "demon" Thomas Sutpen is finally (and literally) mowed down by a man who resembles himself at the beginning of his life—a poor white with no real home. Thus, the story comes full circle, and the dreams of a "grand design" are ended abruptly and violently.

Analysis

This chapter begins with Shreve's narration again, but rapidly changes to Quentin's memory of his father's memory of his grandfather's memory of Thomas Sutpen. Even though this seems confusing, the readers are finally given some real information about the motivation for Thomas Sutpen's monstrous actions, and we are grateful.

Although the story is becoming clearer, Quentin experiences increasing confusion about his own identity. He confuses himself with Shreve and his father, just as Charles Etienne St. Velery Bon is confused about his race, and Thomas Sutpen is confused about his social standing. It is interesting again to note that this confusion may well reflect reality. Faulkner himself grew up in a family much like Quentin Compson's, and his great-grandfather, William

Clarke Falkner, evolved in much the same way as Thomas Sutpen. It's not surprising that the identities are confused in this novel.

The background about Thomas Sutpen clarifies the various paradoxes in the evolution of the Sutpen clan. For instance, Sutpen makes his money from the start by racism. He marries a woman who is the recipient of a plantation fortune. He is surprised to discover that she is part African. Even though Sutpen tries to escape this paradox by repudiating her, his past comes back to haunt him when their son, Charles Bon, turns up at Sutpen's Hundred. When Charles Bon is turned away, recalling the same manner as Thomas Sutpen was turned away from Pettibone's door, the story begins again. There is no ending, only endless cycles of death, murder, and misery in this empire formed on the backs of slaves. The inescapable circularity of history is the ultimate tragedy of the Sutpen clan, and, by extension, it is the tragedy of the American South.

Of all the chapters, Chapter Seven is perhaps the easiest to understand and the most central to the Sutpen myth. Still, it is hard to read. Every time Faulkner gives the reader an edge of understanding the story, he takes it away again, as he brings back his multifaceted stream-of-consciousness narration technique.

Study Questions

1. What are the "dragons' teeth" to which Shreve refers?

2. What further information in Chapter Seven is given about Mr. Coldfield's relationship to Thomas Sutpen?

3. What is Thomas Sutpen's "grand design"?

4. Why won't Thomas Sutpen eat sugar?

5. What was the main event that precipitated Thomas Sutpen's grand design?

6. Why doesn't Thomas Sutpen ever tell the date or the place of his birth?

7. Why was it so difficult for Sutpen's family to follow the pioneer trail west?

8. Why does Thomas Sutpen repudiate his first wife?

9. Where does Thomas Sutpen make his fortune?

10. How does Thomas Sutpen make his fortune?

Answers

1. The "dragons' teeth" that Shreve refers to are the metaphor Mr. Compson uses for Thomas Sutpen's children.

2. Thomas Sutpen persuaded Mr. Coldfield to use his credit in an unethical way to make money, and when the scheme failed, he locked himself in the attic.

3. Thomas Sutpen's grand design is to become a rich plantation owner who sires an empire.

4. Thomas Sutpen won't eat sugar because of the smell of burning sugar in Haiti which was in the air when he defended the Frenchman's plantation against the rebelling slaves.

5. The main event that precipitated Thomas Sutpen's grand design was being turned away from a plantation door by a liveried slave.

6. Thomas Sutpen never tells the date or the place of his birth because he doesn't know them.

7. It was difficult for the family because the mother died and the father was an alcoholic.

8. Thomas Sutpen repudiates his first wife because she was part African.

9. Thomas Sutpen makes his fortune in Haiti.

10. Thomas Sutpen makes his fortune first by being a slave overseer and then by marrying the plantation owner's daughter.

Suggested Essay Topics

1. Describe the motivations for Thomas Sutpen's "grand design" and discuss the reasons for its subsequent failure.

2. During the slavery era in the American South, and after President Lincoln's emancipation proclamation, poor and dispossessed white people could have made common cause with

the black workers who were also in economic peril. Instead, the poor whites identified with the wealthy whites, elevating skin color over economic circumstances. Why? How would history have turned out if poor whites and blacks recognized that they shared common economic interests?

3. When he discovers that his wife has some African ancestry, Sutpen repudiates her. By what logic is some African ancestry enough to make someone black, but some European ancestry is not enough to make someone white? Explain.

4. Describe how the history of the Sutpen clan parallels the history of slavery in the American South.

Chapter 8

New Characters:

Colonel John Sartoris: *a Faulknerian figure, whom Thomas Sutpen replaced as commanding officer in the Civil War*

Colonel Willow: *the man who told Thomas Sutpen that his son Henry was wounded*

Summary

In Chapter Eight, the main remembered "action" of *Absalom, Absalom!* is over. Faulkner has already described Thomas Sutpen's early life, his arrival in Jefferson, his marriage to Ellen Coldfield, the friendship of Henry Sutpen and Charles Bon, the betrothal of Judith Sutpen and Charles Bon, and the two main murders— Henry's murder of Charles Bon, and Wash Jones' murder of Thomas Sutpen. Consequently, Chapter Eight ties up the loose ends of the Sutpen tragedy.

In this chapter the story of Charles Bon is described by Quentin and Shreve in much more detail. Charles Bon grew up in New Orleans, and eventually sought recognition from his father. He befriended Henry Sutpen and gained entry to the Sutpen clan. However, like Thomas Sutpen at Pettibone's gate, he was ultimately denied.

This has implications for Henry as well. Charles must have known who Henry was when he first met him, and plotted to gain admittance to Sutpen's Hundred. Over time, Henry must have also realized this. However, tied to a perverse tradition of honor, he condoned the marriage of siblings, but condemned Charles—and killed him—when he discovered he was one-sixteenth African.

Analysis

The narrative voices in this chapter are still Shreve and Quentin in dialogue, but Quentin is experiencing further difficulty in separating himself from his stories and his surroundings. Faulkner describes it thus:

> "They stared—glared—at one another, their voices (it was Shreve speaking, though save for the slight difference which the intervening degrees of latitude had inculcated in them (differences not in tone or pitch but of turns of phrase and usage of words), it might have been either of them and was in a sense both: both thinking as one, the voice which happened to be speaking the thought only the thinking becoming audible, vocal;..."

Note Faulkner's creative use of punctuation. Here he uses parentheses within parentheses (which are resolved later), dashes, colons, and semi-colons. By the use of this complex system of punctuation, Faulkner is able to recreate the feeling of a mind thinking—when we think, it is in a series of stops and starts, full-and half-thoughts, hopefully returning to the original thought, and making a conclusion.

In this case, Faulkner's conclusion returns us to the basic theme of *Absalom, Absalom!*, which is that of an attempted reconciliation with the ghosts of the past. The sentence continues:

> "the two of them creating between them, out of the rag-tag and bob-ends of old tales and talking, people who perhaps had never existed at all anywhere, who, shadows, were shadows not

of flesh and blood which had lived and died but shadows in turn of what were (to one of them at least, to Shreve) shades too) quiet as the visible murmur of their vaporising breath."

Faulkner gives us no easy answers. He does not say the ghosts are real—they are either shadows or shades or vaporizing breath. In light of the fact that he never allows us consolation or resolution in *Absalom, Absalom!*, it is necessary to know that in *The Sound and the Fury*, published in 1929 (seven years before *Absalom, Absalom!*), Quentin commits suicide in 1910. The questions (and ghosts) are so disturbing to Faulkner's main narrator that he kills himself.

Quentin further confuses his identity (and, by association, Faulkner's identity) with the characters in the story by feeling that Charles and Henry were with them as well: "it was not two but four of them riding the two horses...Charles-Shreve and Quentin-Henry."

The lines between Quentin and Shreve (and, in the previous chapter, between Shreve and Mr. Compson) are blurred. So too are the lines between the various members of the Sutpen clan— Charles, Judith, Henry, Clytie, Charles Etienne, Thomas Sutpen, Jim Bond—all are more related and related in more complex ways to each other than they care to admit. Overall, it is economic classes or racism that causes this confusing division; the background information about Charles Bon serves to underscore the theme of race in *Absalom, Absalom!* Faulkner's view is that racism is a perversion that leads both to the downfall of the Sutpen empire and to the defeat and collapse of the American South.

Study Questions

1. Where is the most contemporary action of *Absalom, Absalom!* taking place?

2. To whom do these words refer: "the two of them creating between them, out of the rag-tag and bob-ends of old tales and talking, people who perhaps had never existed at all anywhere...."?

3. At what university did Henry Sutpen meet Charles Bon?

4. What are the major differences between Henry Sutpen and Charles Bon?

5. How does Quentin further confuse his identity with that of the characters in the story?

6. How does Quentin describe the atmosphere in the Harvard sitting room?

7. How does Shreve describe the Harvard sitting room?

8. Who stopped Quentin from entering the mansion at Sutpen's Hundred?

9. What is the major cause of the fall of the Sutpen empire?

10. Why does Faulkner think the American South is perverse?

Answers

1. The most contemporary action of *Absalom, Absalom!* is taking place in a New England sitting room.

2. These words refer to Quentin and Shreve talking in their sitting room.

3. Henry Sutpen met Charles Bon at the University of Mississippi at Oxford.

4. Henry Sutpen is ten years younger than Charles Bon, and much more naive.

5. Quentin further confuses his identity with the character of Henry; he often notes it was "not two but four of them."

6. Quentin describes the atmosphere in the Harvard sitting room as "tomblike."

7. Shreve describes the Harvard sitting room as a "refrigerator."

8. Clytie stopped Quentin from entering the mansion at Sutpen's Hundred.

9. The major cause of the fall of the Sutpen empire is racism.

10. Faulkner thinks that the American South is perverse because of its history of racism.

Suggested Essay Topics

1. Do you agree with Faulkner's equation of racism and perversity? Use examples from the novel to illustrate your position.

2. As the story reaches its conclusions, the identities of some of the characters blur and blend. At the same time that Faulkner is making one thing clearer, he is making other aspects of the story less clear. What does the author bring to his work by doing this?

3. Offer an interpretation as to why, as the novel gets clearer and clearer, Quentin is confusing his identity more and more with the other characters.

4. In this section of the book, language is again bent beyond its usual shape. Discuss how Faulkner's use of the stream-of-consciousness technique carries the story the last few steps toward its conclusion.

Chapter 9

New Character:

Jim Bond: *"idiot" son of Charles Etienne St. Velery Bon and his African-American wife*

Summary

The narration of the story is concluded. Quentin tells Shreve how Miss Rosa brought him out to Sutpen's Hundred one September and they found Henry still alive, but in hiding. In December, Miss Rosa sends an ambulance, but Clytie thinks that it is a police car and she sets the house on fire, killing herself and Henry.

Now the entire Sutpen clan is destroyed, except for Jim Bond, the "idiot" (who, like Faulkner, gained an extra letter in his last name). Jim Bond stands outside the burning mansion, howling, and then he soon disappears into the woods, still howling. Jim Bond continues to inhabit the woods, and, from time to time, the townspeople of Jefferson can hear him howling.

This is the end result of Thomas Sutpen's "grand design"—a developmentally disabled person howling in the woods. Clearly, it was a design built on faulty premises.

The conclusion of the story prompts Shreve to say that "in time the Jim Bonds are going to conquer the Western Hemisphere." He continues with a philosophical conclusion:

> "Of course it wont quite be in our time and of course as they spread toward the poles they will bleach out again like the rabbits and the birds do, so they wont show up so sharp against the snow. But it will still be Jim Bond; and so in a few thousand years, I who regard you now will also have sprung from the loins of the African kings."

Then Shreve asks Quentin why he hates the South, and Faulkner ends *Absalom, Absalom!* with Quentin shouting to himself "*I dont hate it! I dont hate it!*"

Analysis

In Faulkner's novels, the endings are often very significant to the novel as a whole. Chapter Nine is the final chapter, and Faulkner provides the reader with a revelation and a perverse resolution.

Absalom, Absalom! is the quintessential, if difficult to understand, story of the American South. In it, Thomas Sutpen sets out to create a dynasty for himself, buying slaves and setting himself up as a patriarch. Events take their natural course, and Sutpen's dynasty fails—Quentin, like other young Southerners, is left to pick up the pieces.

In his Nobel-prize acceptance address, Faulkner describes his philosophical understanding of the role of humankind. He sees man as singularly possessing the medium of language, and more specifically, the tirade, with which to immortalize his affairs. He said:

> "It is easy enough to say that man is immortal simply because he will endure: that when the last ding-dong of doom has clanged and faded from the last worthless rock hanging tide-

less in the last red and dying evening, that even then there will still be one more sound: that of his puny, inexhaustible voice, still talking."

In Faulkner's philosophy, language makes man immortal. However, in *Absalom, Absalom!*, the final heir of the Sutpen clan, Jim Bond, is a man without language. Faulkner's message goes further than this. He continues:

"I refuse to accept this. I believe that man will not merely endure: he will prevail. He is immortal, not because he alone among creatures has an inexhaustible voice, but because he has a soul, a spirit capable of compassion and sacrifice and endurance."

In *Absalom, Absalom!*, Faulkner has taken away any easy understandings of life, of morality, or of the soul. In this very difficult novel, he leaves us with an ending that offers no answers.

Perhaps the choice here is similar to that presented in Milton's *Samson Agonistes*. Wrestling with the concept of free will, Samson says "Commands are no constraints. If I obey them, I do it freely..." When Faulkner wrote *Absalom, Absalom!*, he had in mind a tragedy on a grand scale, which meant including the townspeople as a Greek chorus. Since Faulkner viewed *Absalom, Absalom!* as a Greek tragedy, it is useful to look at Milton's description of the genre:

"Tragedy, as it was anciently composed, hath been ever held the gravest, moralest, and most profitable of all other poems: therefore said by Aristotle to be of power, by raising pity and fear, or terror, to purge the mind of those and such like passions, that is, to temper and reduce them to just measure with a kind of delight, stirred up by reading or seeing those passions well imitated."

Here, Milton is paraphrasing a theory begun by Aristotle. Faulkner is continuing in a tradition thousands of years old.

The author's goal in *Absalom, Absalom!,* from this viewpoint, is to bear witness to the machinations of racism and classism within society, to watch the downfall of an immoral man, and to help readers avoid those pitfalls. We, the readers, are meant to align ourselves and our viewpoints with Quentin, and to study the tragedy of the Sutpen clan so that we do not repeat the tragedy of slavery ourselves.

Study Questions

1. Where was Thomas Sutpen born?

2. Where was Faulkner's great-grandfather, William Clark Falkner, born?

3. How old was Thomas Sutpen when he set off to complete his "grand design"?

4. How old was William Clark Falkner when he left his family to make his fortune?

5. In what state of the Union did Thomas Sutpen and William Clark Falkner settle?

6. What role did Thomas Sutpen and William Clark Falkner play in the Civil War?

7. How did Thomas Sutpen and William Clark Falkner finally die?

8. How many children did Thomas Sutpen have?

9. Who is the only surviving member of the Sutpen clan?

10. What is the moral of this story?

Answers

1. Thomas Sutpen was born in the West Virginia mountains.

2. William Clark Falkner was born in the West Virginia mountains.

3. Thomas Sutpen was 14 or 15 when he set off to complete his "grand design."

4. William Clark Falkner was 15 when he left his family to make his fortune.

5. Both Thomas Sutpen and William Clark Falkner settled in Mississippi.

6. Thomas Sutpen and William Clark Falkner were both colonels in the Confederate Army.

7. Thomas Sutpen and William Clark Falkner were both murdered by men who bore them a grudge.

8. Thomas Sutpen had at least five children: Henry, Judith, Charles, Clytie, and Milly's murdered child.

9. The only surviving member of the Sutpen clan is Jim Bond, who is developmentally impaired.

10. The moral of this story is that, if you have children, you'd better recognize them as your own; if you act, you had better recognize your actions as well.

Suggested Essay Topics

1. *Absalom, Absalom!* ends with the main narrator, Quentin, shouting to himself that he does not hate the South. Do you believe that he hates the South, or do you disagree? Why?

2. Why does Shreve McCannon say that the "Jim Bonds" will inherit the earth?

3. One of the major themes of the book can be described as, what comes around goes around. Discuss whether real life does or does not punish people for their sins the way a rough form of justice is meted out in this book.

4. Using the novel and a biography of the author, write an essay charting the parallels between the lives of the characters and Faulkner's family.

Sample Analytical Paper Topics

Topic #1

Discuss the significance of racism to the plot structure of *Absalom, Absalom!*. How did it contribute to the downfall of the Sutpen clan? How was the downfall of the clan foreordained?

Outline

I.   Thesis Statement: *Racism is a central issue to the plot of* Absalom, Absalom! *and contributes to the downfall of Thomas Sutpen's empire.*

II. Outline of Thomas Sutpen's rise:

    A.   Sutpen's humiliation at the Pettibone plantation.

    B.   Sutpen's trip to seek his fortune in Haiti; his role in the Haitian uprising, and his marriage to Eulalia Bon.

    C.   Sutpen's renunciation of Eulalia Bon and their son, Charles Bon.

    D.   Sutpen's building of "Sutpen's Hundred" using slave labor.

III. Ways in which the past returned to haunt Thomas Sutpen:

    A.   His son, Charles Bon, returns and engages himself to Sutpen's daughter, Judith.

    B.   Henry Sutpen chooses friendship with Charles Bon over his relationship with his father.

    C.   Henry kills his friend and his sister's betrothed, Charles Bon.

    D.   Charles Etienne St. Velery Bon appears at Sutpen's Hundred, and acts out the family guilt by marrying a fully-African woman.

    E.   The final child of the clan is not only African, but is also developmentally disabled.

IV.   Conclusion: In Faulkner's view, the Sutpen empire is doomed, due to its basic reliance on an unsustainable economic structure of inequality—likewise the slave economy of the American South was doomed.

Topic #2

People become what they behold, and the ugliness of the American South helped to turn Thomas Sutpen into a brutal man. His deeds are repaid severalfold.

Outline

I.   Thesis Statement: *People raised in a climate of brutality and inhumanity will grow up to emulate what they see, and their actions will be repaid severalfold.*

II.   Examples of humiliation and brutality suffered and inflicted by Sutpen:

    A.   Turned away from the front door of a house by a liveried slave, the young Sutpen learns a lesson about class and status.

    B.   Sutpen resolves that he will be the one dishing out humiliation, not the one who suffers it, even though he is from a poor and alcoholic family.

    C.   Sutpen goes to the West Indies, where fortunes are being made on the backs of slave, he is untroubled by the moral climate, seeing only the possibility of riches.

D. Sutpen buys land and slaves of his own.

III. Examples of the consequences of Sutpen's actions:

    A. Sutpen marries for money and status, but is later driven by racism to abandon his wife.

    B. His son from his marriage resolves to get even.

    C. Sutpen builds an empire, but loses everything.

IV. Conclusion: Raised in a climate of brutality and inhumanity, Sutpen grew up to emulate what he saw, and his actions were repaid.

Topic #3

Discuss how Faulkner uses different modes of narration in order to create a believable yet mythic past.

Outline

I. Thesis Statement: *In* Absalom, Absalom! *Faulkner uses a variety of voices to tell one story. This is specifically a modernist technique, and it works quite well to give shape to a many-faceted story.*

II. Discuss the major narrative voices:

    A. Quentin Compson

    B. Miss Rosa Coldfield

    C. Shreve McCannon

III. Discuss the minor narrative voices:

    A. Mr. Compson

    B. Akers

    C. General Compson

    D. Thomas Sutpen

IV. Establish a theory as to how all these voices work together to tell a story:

    A. How do the voices work in harmony?

B. How do the voices work against each other?

V. Conclusion: The modernist technique of using many different voices to tell a story makes the story harder to understand, but it also makes the story have potential for more (and deeper) meaning.

Topic #4

Miss Rosa's narration of the Sutpen story casts Thomas Sutpen as an evil demon. Write a paper that disagrees with this assumption, and illustrate it using concrete examples from the text.

Outline

I. Thesis Statement: *Despite Miss Rosa's narration (and the narrative of those who know the Sutpen story mainly through Miss Rosa), Thomas Sutpen is not a demon. He was merely a man trying his best to exist in a difficult world.*

II. Miss Rosa is a biased narrator:

A. Miss Rosa's first personal interaction with Thomas Sutpen was one in which she was humiliated by him.

B. Thomas Sutpen was not good to Ellen Sutpen, Miss Rosa's sister, or Goodhue Coldfield, Miss Rosa's father, and thus Miss Rosa would not be inclined to speak well of him.

C. Miss Rosa is a crabby old Southern spinster.

III. Describe the positive things that Thomas Sutpen did in his life:

A. He succeeded in making his fortune, fulfilling a version of the American Dream.

B. He may have owned slaves, but he was intimate with them, too—in fighting and copulation.

C. He built a plantation where there had been only land, thus contributing to the civilization of the world.

D. He provides interesting material for a story.

V. Conclusion: *Absalom, Absalom!* is a story largely presented from a hostile viewpoint. Since most of the narrators are speaking though the sieve of Miss Rosa's memory, the picture that emerges of Thomas Sutpen is unnecessarily negative.

Topic #5

Women are portrayed as being very different in his novel. Sometimes they are weak and sometimes they are strong, but they are close to the center of the story.

Outline

I.   Thesis Statement: *In this novel, women are close to the emotional center of the story.*

II. Examples of women's emotional power:

    A. Miss Rosa's role

        1. Clearly and strongly biased narrator who shapes the story according to memories of events and her feelings.

    B. Sutpen's first wife

        1. Although she is abandoned, her son helps destroy the empire.

III. Examples of women's actions:

    A. The strength of the love felt by the women for their friends and suitors.

    B. Clytie is scared, but she acts—and burns down the house.

IV. Conclusion: Even when they are not directly making things happen, women are never far from the emotional center of the story.

SECTION FOUR

Bibliography

Quotations from *Absalom, Absalom!* are taken from the following edition:

Faulkner, William. *Absalom, Absalom!: The Corrected Text.* First published 1936, corrected 1986. New York: Vintage Books, 1990.

Other works consulted:

Abrams, M. H. *The Norton Anthology of English Literature.* New York: W. W. Norton & Company, 1986.

Blotner, Joseph. *Faulkner: A Biography.* New York: Vintage Books, 1991.

Cowley, Malcolm. *The Portable Faulkner.* New York: Viking Press, 1967.

Available at your local bookstore or order directly from us by sending in coupon below.

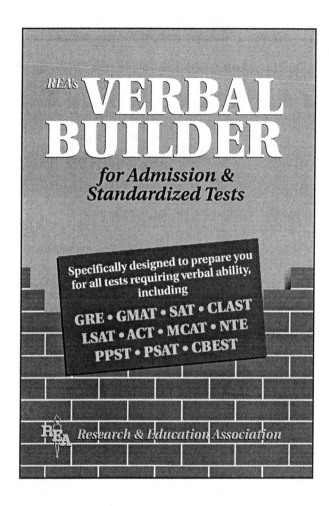

MAXnotes®

REA's Literature Study Guides

MAXnotes® are student-friendly. They offer a fresh look at masterpieces of literature, presented in a lively and interesting fashion. **MAXnotes®** offer the essentials of what you should know about the work, including outlines, explanations and discussions of the plot, character lists, analyses, and historical context. **MAXnotes®** are designed to help you think independently about literary works by raising various issues and thought-provoking ideas and questions. Written by literary experts who currently teach the subject, **MAXnotes®** enhance your understanding and enjoyment of the work.

Available **MAXnotes®** include the following:

Absalom, Absalom!
The Aeneid of Virgil
Animal Farm
Antony and Cleopatra
As I Lay Dying
As You Like It
The Autobiography of
    Malcolm X
The Awakening
Beloved
Beowulf
Billy Budd
The Bluest Eye, A Novel
Brave New World
The Canterbury Tales
The Catcher in the Rye
The Color Purple
The Crucible
Death in Venice
Death of a Salesman
The Divine Comedy I: Inferno
Dubliners
Emma
Euripedes' Electra & Medea
Frankenstein
Gone with the Wind
The Grapes of Wrath
Great Expectations
The Great Gatsby
Gulliver's Travels
Hamlet
Hard Times

Heart of Darkness
Henry IV, Part I
Henry V
The House on Mango Street
Huckleberry Finn
I Know Why the Caged
    Bird Sings
The Iliad
Invisible Man
Jane Eyre
Jazz
The Joy Luck Club
Jude the Obscure
Julius Caesar
King Lear
Les Misérables
Lord of the Flies
Macbeth
The Merchant of Venice
The Metamorphoses of Ovid
The Metamorphosis
Middlemarch
A Midsummer Night's Dream
Moby-Dick
Moll Flanders
Mrs. Dalloway
Much Ado About Nothing
My Antonia
Native Son
1984
The Odyssey
Oedipus Trilogy

Of Mice and Men
On the Road
Othello
Paradise Lost
A Passage to India
Plato's Republic
Portrait of a Lady
A Portrait of the Artist
    as a Young Man
Pride and Prejudice
A Raisin in the Sun
Richard II
Romeo and Juliet
The Scarlet Letter
Sir Gawain and the
    Green Knight
Slaughterhouse-Five
Song of Solomon
The Sound and the Fury
The Stranger
The Sun Also Rises
A Tale of Two Cities
Taming of the Shrew
The Tempest
Tess of the D'Urbervilles
Their Eyes Were Watching God
To Kill a Mockingbird
To the Lighthouse
Twelfth Night
Uncle Tom's Cabin
Waiting for Godot
Wuthering Heights